Sharp Image Company in asso
and Neil McPherson for the Fir
by arrangement with Playmar

The European premiere

ANAHERA
by Emma Kinane

FINBOROUGH | THEATRE
VIBRANT **NEW WRITING** | UNIQUE **REDISCOVERIES**

First performed at the Finborough Theatre as a staged reading as part of
Vibrant 2018 – A Festival of Finborough Playwrights: Thursday, 25 October 2018.
First performance at the Finborough Theatre: Tuesday, 3 September 2019.

Anahera received development assistance from Auckland Theatre Company, New Zealand, as part of Next Stage 2015.

ANAHERA
by Emma Kinane

Cast in order of speaking

Liz	**Caroline Faber**
Anahera	**Acushla-Tara Kupe**
Peter	**Rupert Wickham**
Imogen	**Jessica O'Toole**
Harry	**Paul Waggott**

The play is set in New Zealand/Aotearoa in two time periods, twenty years apart – ten years in the past and ten years in the future. The future scenes run in reverse order chronologically.

The performance lasts approximately two hours and fifteen minutes.

There will be one interval of fifteen minutes.

Director	**Alice Kornitzer**
Designer	**Emily Bestow**
Lighting Designer	**Gregory Jordan**
Composer	**Kate Marlais**
Movement Director	**Natasha Warder**
Producer	**Claire Evans**
Associate Producer	**CJ Bailey**

Please turn your mobile phones off – the light they emit can also be distracting.

Our patrons are respectfully reminded that, in this intimate theatre, any noise such as the rustling of programmes, food packaging or talking may distract the actors and your fellow audience members.

We regret there is no admittance or re-admittance to the auditorium whilst the performance is in progress.

Caroline Faber | Liz

Productions at the Finborough Theatre include *Hangover Square*.

Theatre includes *Network*, *The Heiress* (National Theatre), *Romeo and Juliet*, *Paradise Lost* (Headlong), *King Lear* (The Young Vic), *In Lipstick* (Pleasance Edinburgh), *The Iliad* (Almeida Theatre)*, The Taming of The Shrew*, *Edward III*, *The Malcontent*, *Here Lies Mary Spindler*, *Keepers of The Flame* (Royal Shakespeare Company), *My Mother Said I Never Should* (St James Theatre), *Piaf* (Octagon Theatre, Bolton), *Othello*, *Macbeth* (Lyric Theatre, Hammersmith), *The Norman Conquests*, *Last Easter* (Birmingham Repertory Theatre), *Dangerous Corner* (Garrick Theatre), *Tender, Luna Gale* (Hampstead Theatre), *The Colonel Bird* (Gate Theatre), *Kanye the First* (HighTide Festival), *The Mill on the Floss* (New Ambassadors Theatre and National Tour for Shared Experience), *The End of the Affair* (Bridewell Theatre), *Vermillion Dream*, *Top Girls*, *The Merchant of Venice* (Salisbury Playhouse) and *Cavalcade* (Sadler's Wells Theatre).

Television includes *Berlin Station*, *Merlin*, *Midsomer Murders*, *Foyle's War*, *EastEnders*, *A Good Murder*, *My Spy Family*, *Casualty*, *Holby City*, *The Bill* and *Gamesmaster*.

Acushla-Tara Kupe *Ngāti Maniapoto* | Anahera

Productions at the Finborough Theatre include *Anahera* as part of *Vibrant 2018 – A Festival of Finborough Playwrights* and *Astroman* as part of *Vibrant 2019 – A Festival of Finborough Playwrights.*

Theatre includes *A View From the Bridge*, *Kings of the Gym* (Circa Theatre, Wellington), *2080*, *Spring Awakening* (BATS Theatre), *Like You Hate Me* (Lion and Unicorn Theatre), *Romeo and Juliet* (Mayhem Theatre), *The Sea Queen* and *Twelfth Night* (London Free Open Air Theatre Season), *Hotel and Salon* (New Zealand National Tour), *They Have Long Arms and They Can Find Me* (Katzpace).

Film includes *Fresh Meat*, *Chronesthesia*, *Encounters*, *Woman in Blue*, *The Return*, *Lantana* and *The Practitioner*.

Television includes *Creeped Out*.

Radio includes *The Christchurch Murder* and *The Offensive Podcast*.

Acushla-Tara is a member of the all-female Shakespeare company Dangerous Space and performs across Europe with the London Māori Club Ngāti Rānana.

Jessica O'Toole | Imogen

Trained at Royal Central School of Speech and Drama.

Theatre includes *She's Not There* (White Bear Theatre), *Split Ends* and *The Memory of Water* (Jermyn Street Theatre), *What Some People Do* (Lyric Theatre, Hammersmith) and *King John* (Tour).

Film includes *Morning Song*, *Remember Me*, *Pet Graveyard*, *End Game*, *Pagan Warrior* and *Scarecrow's Revenge*.

Television includes *Bridgerton*, *A Place of Safety* and *Rules of Love*.

Radio includes *The Write Hour*.

Paul Waggott | Harry

Productions at the Finborough Theatre include *Astroman* as part of *Vibrant 2019 – A Festival of Finborough Playwrights.*

Trained at Victoria University of Wellington, graduating with a BA (Hons) in Theatre.

Theatre includes *The Road That Wasn't There* (New Zealand National Tour), *Joseph* (BATS Theatre), *A View from the Bridge*, *Red* (Circa Theatre and National Theatre of New Zealand).

Film includes *Causims* and *Chronesthesia*.

Radio includes *The Offensive*, *Wulf* and *The Witching Hours*.

Rupert Wickham | Peter

Productions at the Finborough Theatre include *Imaginationship*.

Trained at the Royal Central School of Speech and Drama.

Theatre includes *Stalin's Favourite* (National Tour), *Private Lives* (Nottingham Playhouse), *Defying Hitler* (National Tour and 59E59 Theaters, New York City), *Quartermaine's Terms* (Salisbury Playhouse), *Journey's End* (Comedy Theatre), *Henry V* (National Theatre), *The Winslow Boy* (Chichester Festival Theatre and National Tour), *Not About Heroes* (National Tour), *Death and the Maiden* (King's Head Theatre), *Othello* (National Tour), *Hamlet* (Greenwich Theatre), *King Lear* (Ludlow Festival), *Romeo and Juliet* (Open Air Theatre, Regent's Park) and *The Importance of Being Earnest* (Royal Exchange Theatre, Manchester).

Film includes *Journey's End*, *Woman in Gold*, *Mission Impossible 5*, *Stand Off* and *The Bourne Identity*.

Television includes *Silk*, *The Spacerace*, *Waking the Dead*, *A Dance to the Music of Time* and *Band of Brothers*.

Radio includes *Betsie and the Emperor* and *Poetry Please*.

Emma Kinane | Playwright

Emma Kinane is an award winning writer and actor. She is a graduate of Toi Whakaari: New Zealand Drama School and has worked as an actor, writer and director in theatre, television, film and radio. She has a Master's Degree in Scriptwriting from the International Institute of Modern Letters at Victoria University.

Her writing includes co-writing the plays *Turbine*, *Paua* and *The December Brother* with the SEEyD Collective, radio play *Clouds,* which aired on Radio NZ in 2014, and short film *Bastard*, part of the 2018 anthology feature *Encounters*.

Her latest play *Micronation Street* recently had a workshop and rehearsed reading at Circa Theatre, Wellington.

Alice Kornitzer | Director

Trained at the Berliner Ensemble, Germany and University of Bristol where she gained a BA (Hons) in Drama.

Direction includes *Chummy* which was nominated for four Off West End Awards including Best Director (White Bear Theatre), *Wuthering Heights* (National Tour), *Apocalypse Laow* (Katzspace), *Sir Walter's Women* (The Great Hall, Winchester, for Hampshire Heritage Trust), *The Taming of the Shrew* (Petersfield Shakespeare Festival and Theatre Royal Winchester), *Tejas Verdes* (The Court Theatre Training Company), *Broke Britannia* (Bridewell Theatre) and *The Accidental Caregiver* (Robert Moss Theatre, New York City).

Assistant Direction and Dramaturgy includes *Die Präsidentin* (Theater Magdeburg), *Happy New* (Trafalgar Studios), *Tejas Verdes* and *Allotment* (Edinburgh Fringe Festival), and *Das Fieber* (Theater Unterm Dach, Berlin).

She was also the recipient of the 2018 European Theatre Conference Artist Residency Award.

Emily Bestow | Designer

Theatre includes *The Marvelous Wonderettes* (Upstairs at the Gatehouse and Theatre Royal Windsor), *Honk! The Musical* (National Tour and Union Theatre), *Cry Havoc* (Park Theatre), *Red Riding Hood Versus The Wolf* (Stantonbury Theatre), *Cry God, for Harry England and St George!* (Duke of York's Theatre and Edinburgh Fringe Festival), *Flat Out, Top Hat, Treating Odette, Anything Goes, Wallis: A Certain Person* and *The MGM Story* (Upstairs at the Gatehouse), *A Little Night Music, Absurd Person Singular and The 39 Steps* (Frinton Summer Theatre), *Beauty and the Beast* (Magdalen College School), *Pete 'n' Keely* (Tristan Bates Theatre), *Princess Suffragette* (The Vaults) and *Broke Britannia!* (The Bridewell Centre).

As Design Assistant to Anna Fleischle, Emily worked on *A Very, Very, Very Dark Matter* (Bridge Theatre), *The Way of the World* (Donmar Warehouse), *Home, I'm Darling* (Theatr Clwyd and National Theatre) and *The Writer* (Almeida Theatre).

Gregory Jordan | Lighting Designer

Productions at the Finborough Theatre include *Cyril's Success* and *Veterans Day*.

Trained at Rose Bruford College and holds a BA (Hons) in Lighting Design.

Lighting Designs include *The Hunchback of Notre Dame* (Iris Theatre), *Red Ribbons* (Les Enfants Terrible), *Mess* (The Other Palace), *Goodnight Mr Tom* (Southwark Playhouse), *The Enchanted* (Bunker Theatre), *Breakfast* (The Vaults), *Island Song* (Nursery Theatre), *Spring Awakening* and *Little Women* (Stockwell Playhouse), *Sister Act The Musical* (KD Theatre Productions), *The Wizard of Oz* (National Tour), *Killymuck* (National Tour) and *Lemons* (Barons Court Theatre).

Other work includes on *The Wolf of Wall Street, Coma* (Stratton Oakmont Productions), *Equus* (Theatre Royal Stratford East and National Tour), *The Divine Proportions* (The Vaults), *Schism* (Park Theatre), *The Great Gatsby* (Gatsby's Drugstore), *The Phantom of the Opera* (Her Majesty's Theatre), *Urinetown* (Apollo Theatre) and *Accolade* (St. James Theatre).

Kate Marlais | Composer

Kate Marlais has a Bachelor of Music degree with Composition major from King's College London and studied Musical Theatre at the Royal Academy of Music, where she was recently made Associate (ARAM) for her work in music.

She was the 2018-19 Cameron Mackintosh Resident Composer at Lyric Theatre, Hammersmith.

Her work as a Composer includes *Abandon* (Lyric Theatre, Hammersmith) for which she was nominated for Best Composer at the Stage Debut Awards 2018, *Hear Her Song* (International Tour for The Canales Project and UN Decade of Women) and *Rare Birds* (Soho Theatre).

As Co-Writer and Co-Composer, her work includes *Here* for which she won the 2015 S and S award and *F**ked in Marrakech* (BEAM Festival at Theatre Royal Stratford East).

Musical Direction, Music Production for Stage, Musical Arranging and Vocal Coaching includes *Musik* (Assembly Rooms, Edinburgh and Leicester Square Theatre), *Chorus of Others* (Frantic Assembly's platform at the National Theatre River Stage), *Princess* (National Theatre River Stage), *Leave To Remain* (Lyric Theatre, Hammersmith), *For You I Long the Longest* (National Tour), *Tesco 100 Years' Choir* (Birmingham NEC), *Fatherland* (Lyric Theatre, Hammersmith, and Royal Exchange Theatre, Manchester).

Kate is the Founder of *Modulate*, a platform and initiative for female identifying composers for the UK stage.

Natasha Warder | Movement Director

Trained in Contemporary Dance and Physical Theatre at the School of Theatre and Dance at San Francisco State University, San Francisco, and an MSc in writing at the University of Edinburgh.

Movement Direction includes *Cherry* (ODC Theater, San Francisco) and *Woman/Sleeps* (PTC, Berlin).

Theatre includes *Every Brilliant Thing* (Cockpit Theatre), *Not in The Picture* (CounterPULSE), and *Alsomitra* (Malleble Dance Theatre).

Laura Clifford | Assistant Director

Theatre includes *Entropy* (Underbelly, Edinburgh, and White Bear Theatre) and *The Monkey's Paw* (Bread and Roses Theatre), where she was Associate Emerging Director in 2017. She has assisted on *The Art of Gaman* (Theatre503) and has directed at *Rapid Wright Response* nights.

Claire Evans | Producer

Productions at the Finborough include *Me and Juliet*, *Bed and Sofa* and *Astroman* as part of *Vibrant – A Festival of Finborough Playwrights 2019*.

Claire read English and Drama at Royal Holloway College and has worked as a director, producer and theatrical agent.

Direction includes *Belle Fontaine* (The Vaults), Paul Taylor Mills' summer play festivals at the Theatre Royal Windsor, the Pomegranate Theatre, Chesterfield and the Manor Pavilion Theatre, Sidmouth, and a play-reading of *LAZYeye* (Above The Arts Theatre).

Producing and co-producing work includes *King John* and *Fair Em* (Union Theatre), *Bette Davis On The Edge* (National Tour), *Ladylogue* (Tristan Bates Theatre) and *By My Strength* (Women and War Festival, London).

She was also Production Co-ordinator for the MTFestUK festival of new musical theatre (The Other Palace), and is currently Production Co-ordinator for *Torch Song* (Turbine Theatre, Battersea).

CJ Bailey | Associate Producer

Trained as an operatic soprano, and has worked as an opera singer, producer and librettist.

Operas produced include Wagner's *Parsifal*, *Truncated Tristan* and *A Midsummer Night's Wet Dream* (Off Colour Opera), which they co-created and co-wrote. CJ also produced *Lipstick: A Fairy Tale of Modern Iran* (Omnibus Theatre as part of the '96 Festival, Clapham).

Other work includes running an opera company Telescopera, presenting *Truncated Tristan* and *Parsikure*.

CJ is also developing a new opera with Shatterbeam Productions.

Production Acknowledgements

Casting Director
Aurora Causin

Assistant Director
Laura Clifford

Cover Image of Acushla-Tara Kupe
Tabitha Arthur Photography

Cover Graphic Design
Arsalan Sattari

Rehearsal Photographer
Alain Landes

Fundraising and
Production Assistance
Rosie Flood
Maria Majewska
Karina Patel

Thanks to Murray Lynch at Playmarket New Zealand.

Anahera has been funded through generous donations made as part of Anahera's Crowdfunding campaign.

FINBOROUGH | THEATRE

VIBRANT **NEW WRITING** | UNIQUE **REDISCOVERIES**

118 Finborough Road, London SW10 9ED

admin@finboroughtheatre.co.uk | www.finboroughtheatre.co.uk

"Probably the most influential fringe theatre in the world."
Time Out

"Under Neil McPherson, possibly the most unsung of all major artistic directors in Britain, the Finborough has continued to plough a fertile path of new plays and rare revivals that gives it an influence disproportionate to its tiny 50-seat size."
Mark Shenton, *The Stage*

"The mighty little Finborough which, under Neil McPherson, continues to offer a mixture of neglected classics and new writing in a cannily curated mix."
Lyn Gardner, *The Stage*

"The tiny but mighty Finborough"
Ben Brantley, *The New York Times*

Founded in 1980, the multi-award-winning Finborough Theatre presents plays and music theatre, concentrated exclusively on vibrant new writing and unique rediscoveries from the 19th and 20th centuries.

Our programme is unique – we never present work that has been seen anywhere in London during the last 25 years. Behind the scenes, we continue to discover and develop a new generation of theatre makers – most notably through our annual festival of new writing, now in its eleventh consecutive year – *Vibrant – A Festival of Finborough Playwrights*.

Despite remaining completely unsubsidised, the Finborough Theatre has an unparalleled track record for attracting the finest talent who go on to become leading voices in British theatre. Under Artistic Director Neil McPherson, it has discovered some of the UK's most exciting new playwrights including Laura Wade, James Graham, Mike Bartlett, Jack Thorne, Alexandra Wood, Nicholas de Jongh and Anders Lustgarten; and directors including Tamara Harvey, Robert Hastie, Blanche McIntyre, Kate Wasserberg and Sam Yates.

Artists working at the theatre in the 1980s included Clive Barker, Rory Bremner, Nica Burns, Kathy Burke, Ken Campbell, Jane Horrocks and Claire Dowie. In the 1990s, the Finborough Theatre first became known for new writing including Naomi Wallace's first play *The War Boys*; Rachel Weisz in David Farr's *Neville Southall's Washbag*; four plays by Anthony Neilson including *Penetrator* and *The Censor*, both of which transferred to the Royal Court Theatre; and new plays by Richard Bean, Lucinda Coxon, David Eldridge, Tony Marchant and Mark Ravenhill. New writing development included the premieres of modern classics such as Mark Ravenhill's *Shopping and F***king*, Conor McPherson's *This Lime Tree Bower*, Naomi Wallace's *Slaughter City* and Martin McDonagh's *The Pillowman*.

Since 2000, new British plays have included Laura Wade's London debut *Young Emma*, commissioned for the Finborough Theatre; two one-woman shows by Miranda Hart; James Graham's *Albert's Boy* with Victor Spinetti; Sarah Grochala's *S27*; Athena Stevens' *Schism* which was nominated for an Olivier Award; and West End transfers for Joy Wilkinson's *Fair*; Nicholas de Jongh's *Plague Over England*; Jack Thorne's *Fanny and Faggot*; Neil McPherson's Olivier Award nominated *It Is Easy To Be Dead*; and Dawn King's *Foxfinder*.

UK premieres of foreign plays have included plays by Brad Fraser, Lanford Wilson, Larry Kramer, Tennessee Williams, the English premiere of Robert McLellan's Scots language classic, *Jamie the Saxt*; and three West End transfers – Frank McGuinness' *Gates of Gold* with William Gaunt and John Bennett; and Craig Higginson's *Dream of the Dog* with Dame Janet Suzman.

Rediscoveries of neglected work – most commissioned by the Finborough Theatre – have included the first London revivals of Rolf Hochhuth's *Soldiers* and *The Representative*; both parts of Keith Dewhurst's *Lark Rise to Candleford*; *The Women's War*, an evening of original suffragette plays; *Etta Jenks* with Clarke Peters and Daniela Nardini; Noël Coward's first play *The Rat Trap*; Emlyn Williams' *Accolade*; Lennox Robinson's *Drama at Inish* with Celia Imrie and Paul O'Grady; John Van Druten's *London Wall* which transferred to St James' Theatre; and J. B. Priestley's *Cornelius* which transferred to a sell out Off Broadway run in New York City.

Music Theatre has included the new (premieres from Grant Olding, Charles Miller, Michael John LaChuisa, Adam Guettel, Andrew Lippa, Paul Scott Goodman, and Adam Gwon's *Ordinary Days* which transferred to the West End) and the old (the UK premiere of Rodgers and Hammerstein's *State Fair* which also transferred to the West End), and the acclaimed 'Celebrating British Music Theatre' series.

The Finborough Theatre won *The Stage* Fringe Theatre of the Year Award in 2011, *London Theatre Reviews'* Empty Space Peter Brook Award in 2010 and 2012, swept the board with eight awards at the 2012 OffWestEnd Awards, and was nominated for an Olivier Award in 2017 and 2019. Artistic Director Neil McPherson was awarded the Critics' Circle Special Award for Services to Theatre in 2019.

It is the only unsubsidised theatre ever to be awarded the Channel 4 Playwrights Scheme bursary eleven times.

www.finboroughtheatre.co.uk

Supported by

Mailing
Email admin@finboroughtheatre.co.uk or give your details to our Box Office staff to join our free email list.

Feedback
We welcome your comments, complaints and suggestions. Write to Finborough Theatre, 118 Finborough Road, London SW10 9ED or email us at admin@finboroughtheatre.co.uk

Playscripts
Many of the Finborough Theatre's plays have been published and are on sale from our website.

On Social Media

 www.facebook.com/FinboroughTheatre

 www.twitter.com/finborough

 finboroughtheatre.tumblr.com

 www.instagram.com/finboroughtheatre

 www.youtube.com/user/finboroughtheatre

Friends
The Finborough Theatre is a registered charity. We receive no public funding, and rely solely on the support of our audiences. Please do consider supporting us by becoming a member of our Friends of the Finborough Theatre scheme. There are four categories of Friends, each offering a wide range of benefits.

Richard Tauber Friends – David and Melanie Alpers. David Barnes. Mark Bentley. Kate Beswick. Deirdre Feehan. Michael Forster. Jennifer Jacobs. Paul and Lindsay Kennedy. Martin and Wendy Kramer. John Lawson. Kathryn McDowall.

William Terriss Friends – Paul Guinery. Janet and Leo Liebster. Ros and Alan Haigh.

Adelaide Neilson Friends – Philip G Hooker.

The Steam Industry was founded by Phil Willmott in 1992. It comprises two strands to its work: the Finborough Theatre (under Artistic Director Neil McPherson); and The Phil Willmott Company (under Artistic Director Phil Willmott) which presents productions throughout London as well as annually at the Finborough Theatre.

Emma Kinane

ANAHERA

OBERON BOOKS
LONDON

WWW.OBERONBOOKS.COM

First published in 2019 by Oberon Books Ltd
521 Caledonian Road, London N7 9RH
Tel: +44 (0) 20 7607 3637 / Fax: +44 (0) 20 7607 3629
e-mail: info@oberonbooks.com
www.oberonbooks.com

PB ISBN:9781786829979
E ISBN: 9781786829986

Cover: Image of Acushla-Tara Kupe by Tabitha Arthur Photography,
and Graphic Design by Arsalan Sattari

Printed and bound by 4EDGE Limited, Hockley, Essex, UK.
eBook conversion by Lapiz Digital Services, India.

Characters

ANAHERA   *23, newly qualified social worker*
LIZ   *37, high-flying public servant*
PETER   *37, self-employed businessman*

In the future scenes, Liz and Peter's adult children:

HARRY   *31, chef, divorced, parent of two*
IMOGEN   *28, post-grad student, caregiver*

Setting:
The play is set in two time periods 20 years apart; 10 years in the past and 10 years in the future. The future scenes run in reverse order chronologically.

Anahera received development assistance from Auckland Theatre Company, New Zealand as part of Next Stage 2015. First production at Circa Theatre, Wellington, New Zealand on 9 September 2017 with the following cast:

LIZ: Jacqueline Nairn
ANAHERA: Neenah Dekkers-Reihana
PETER: Neill Rea
IMOGEN: Susie Berry
HARRY: Simon Leary

Creative Team
Director: Katie Wolfe
Set Design: Mark McEntyre
Lighting Design: Lisa Maule
Costume Design: Tania Klouwens
Sound Design: Andrew McMillan & Katie Wolfe

Act One

SCENE PAST ONE: HARRY IS MISSING. FIRST SUSPICIONS.

10am April 10 years ago

LIZ and PETER's lounge. There are no children's toys; it's a very adult space, very clean, super tidy, expensive décor.

ANAHERA sits on the couch with official-looking papers on her lap. PETER paces up and down near the window. LIZ sits in a chair, blank. There is a tray with an empty pot of coffee and four empty cups. They've been here for a while.

There is a long silence as they wait.

ANAHERA fumbles and drops some papers on the floor. She scoops them up, but then drops her pen.

PETER moves around the room, fiddling with ornaments, unable to keep still.

LIZ hears something.

LIZ: Is that…?

> *They all listen.*

> *Nothing. LIZ slumps, PETER paces.*

ANAHERA: They'll find him, Liz.

PETER: They'd find him faster if they'd let me help.

ANAHERA: I know it's hard, but this really is the best way.

PETER: How would you know? What are you, three?

LIZ: Peter.

ANAHERA: It's okay. I understand.

PETER: Sorry. I'm not…

ANAHERA: I know. It's okay.

A silence. ANAHERA puts her notes to one side and focuses on LIZ and PETER. She is nervous and excited – this is her first time solo – but she is also competent and empathetic.

ANAHERA: Why don't we try and find that photo they asked for.

PETER: With the clothes.

ANAHERA: Yes, the clothes he was wearing.

PETER goes to LIZ's bag, gets out her Blackberry and takes it to her. She searches through the photos on the phone.

ANAHERA: I know it's hard, but you're doing everything right, and it's just a matter of time now. We just have to wait.

LIZ: How long?

ANAHERA: They're following a very specific protocol which –

A reminder comes up on LIZ's phone.

LIZ: I should be in a meeting. *(Immediately backtracking.)* That sounded – *(wrong.)* I mean, I'm not sure how much more… *(I can take.)*

LIZ looks to PETER. He comes over and holds her, taking her phone and putting it down on the table.

ANAHERA: Liz, I understand how difficult this is, but they're mobilising all sorts of people and resources, and it takes a little time, that's all.

A silence.

ANAHERA remembers the next item on her mental list.

2

ANAHERA: Would you like me to phone someone?

LIZ and PETER don't answer.

ANAHERA: The people who picked up Imogen? Are they friends of yours?

PETER: Just parents – Imi goes to school with their kid.

A beat. LIZ disengages from PETER, grabs a tissue and blows her nose.

ANAHERA: Is there someone else? Family maybe?

LIZ: Your name. It means angel, doesn't it?

ANAHERA: Do you speak te reo?

LIZ: No. Great name for a social worker.

ANAHERA: Thanks.

LIZ: Do you come from around here?

ANAHERA: No. Is there someone else I can call? Someone from your church? You can't have too many people around you at a time like this.

LIZ: Not yet. Where are you from?

LIZ looks pleadingly at ANAHERA. ANAHERA relents.

ANAHERA: I'm from Whanganui.

LIZ: Nice. I always feel like I'm on holiday in Whanganui. Would you like some cake, Anahera?

ANAHERA: That would be lovely.

No-one moves to get the cake.

LIZ: I made a carrot cake last night. It was Harry's turn to lick the bowl.

3

LIZ stops. PETER looks away. ANAHERA tries to keep the conversation going.

ANAHERA: Is that his favourite?

LIZ: What?

ANAHERA: Is carrot cake his favourite?

LIZ: His favourite? I don't... *(know.)* Does it matter?

PETER: Of course not! They're not going to lure him back with his favourite cake, are they?

A silence.

PETER: The woman who was here before, your boss.

ANAHERA: My colleague. Janet.

PETER: Is she coming back?

ANAHERA: As soon as she can.

LIZ and PETER glance at each other. ANAHERA notices.

ANAHERA: She wouldn't have left if it wasn't an emergency. Other than... the emergency, Harry is our highest priority.

PETER: What's happened?

ANAHERA: Don't worry about that.

PETER: But if –

ANAHERA: I'm sorry, it's confidential.

LIZ: Is it Harry?

ANAHERA: No, I promise. Nothing to do with Harry. Janet will be back as soon as she can and I will stay as long as you need me. Alright?

LIZ nods.

4

PETER: Thanks.

ANAHERA: Let's find that photo.

ANAHERA picks up LIZ's Blackberry and hands it to LIZ.

ANAHERA: You keep looking and I'll put the kettle on again. I'll only be a minute.

ANAHERA leaves the room.

LIZ searches through the photos. PETER paces again.

LIZ's searching slows. Stops.

LIZ: I feel ill.

PETER: I know.

LIZ: No, I mean sick. Like I could vomit.

PETER: Should I get a bucket?

LIZ: No.

PETER: *(about the photos)* I'll do it, love.

PETER takes the phone and begins to swipe through photos.

LIZ looks at PETER intensely.

LIZ: I want him back.

PETER: *(distracted)* Me too.

LIZ: No, you don't... *(understand.)* It's different. I didn't realise that - It's like my leg's been amputated and I'm not sure I'll be able to walk without it.

PETER: Oh, love.

LIZ: Like something vital is missing.

PETER: I know.

LIZ: No, you're not... *(listening.)* I didn't realise it was vital. I didn't know I would feel like... It's like I've bumped my knee but my ear is hurting. Do you... *(know what I mean?)*

PETER: No.

LIZ: It's different, not what I was -

PETER: You never had a child go missing before, you didn't know how it would feel.

LIZ: No, you still don't - *(understand.)* I didn't think I would feel - *(anything.)*

LIZ stops talking because she doesn't want to go there.

PETER holds the phone out, showing LIZ a photo. She nods.

He tries to reassure her she's done nothing wrong.

PETER: What happened? Last night. Did he do something?

LIZ: I've already said, there was nothing -

PETER: Yeah, but -

LIZ: No, no "buts", nothing happened, that's why it doesn't make sense.

PETER: You shouldn't feel guilty. If nothing happened.

LIZ: He just looked at me. He stood in the kitchen doorway and looked at me.

She claws her way out of the horrible feelings and heads to her safe place – anger. Her anger slowly builds, but she covers it.

ANAHERA comes back in.

ANAHERA: I forgot to ask, does Harry - ?

PETER hands her the phone.

PETER: That's the top he was wearing last night.

ANAHERA: That's a great photo. Really clear. Good choice. Can we email it to Janet? She'll forward it to the sergeant.

ANAHERA doesn't know how to use a Blackberry. LIZ takes the phone from her.

LIZ: What's her address?

ANAHERA scrabbles around in her bag, finds Janet's business card and offers it. LIZ takes the card and walks away, entering the email address into her phone.

ANAHERA: It might be good to offer a second choice, just in case.

PETER: That's really the only one. Only recent one.

ANAHERA is surprised, but tries not to show it.

ANAHERA: Okay.

LIZ screws up the card and drops it on the sideboard. She emails the photo.

PETER: Sorry, I interrupted you.

ANAHERA: Oh, does Harry do any after school activities - cubs or sports, something where he has a different group of friends who might know where he is?

PETER: The police already asked that.

LIZ: Waste of time.

PETER: Liz.

LIZ: He'll come back when he's hungry.

PETER: What if he's hurt? Trapped somewhere? He's never done anything like this before.

LIZ: He's changing. Pushing the boundaries.

ANAHERA: Well, teenage brains are -

PETER: *(to Anahera)* He's not a bad kid.

ANAHERA: Their brains don't work in the same way as -

LIZ: He's not a teenager yet, he's just a kid.

ANAHERA: Is he angry with you about something?

LIZ: He's an 11 year old boy. They all think they're owed the
world.

ANAHERA: Is that what Harry thinks?

LIZ: Harry doesn't think. He was cross, he ran away, that's all.
Everyone's overreacting. Didn't you run away when you
were a kid?

ANAHERA: No.

LIZ: Really?

ANAHERA: Really.

LIZ takes a moment to breathe.

LIZ: I'm sorry.

ANAHERA: It's okay.

PETER: It's okay, love.

PETER puts his arms around her.

ANAHERA: The police have got every available person
looking for him. They'll find him.

LIZ: I'm grateful. I know I don't sound it, but...

PETER: *(to Anahera)* Thanks for believing. It helps.

ANAHERA: It's more than belief. In these situations -

LIZ: Māori are very spiritual, aren't they?

ANAHERA: I was going to say, it's statistically in your favour. About 98% of kids show up within a day.

LIZ: Sorry. I didn't mean to offend.

ANAHERA: You didn't. *(She did.)* Most people are spiritual, aren't they, in their own way?

LIZ grasps the subject – anything to distract herself. She breaks away from PETER.

LIZ: There are differences – a different awareness, different expectations. I read about a doctor who was also a clairvoyant and he said he'd never had a Māori patient come to an appointment alone, and he wasn't talking about the living. There were always random people standing round the edge of the room; watching, supporting, even if the patient had no idea they were there. I think that's beautiful. And sad for the ones who are alone. The Pākehā.

PETER: We're not alone.

LIZ: I'm not talking about religion.

PETER: Nor am I. I'm talking about us.

LIZ and PETER have a moment of connection. PETER breaks it first, a little uncomfortable with ANAHERA there, even though ANAHERA has tactfully looked away.

PETER: Sorry. We're...

ANAHERA: You're supporting each other. Some people can't do that in times of stress, they turn away from each other.

PETER: I suppose you see a lot of bad relationships in your job. Does it make you cynical?

LIZ: She's too young to be cynical.

PETER: How old are you?

ANAHERA: Can I just reframe that? In terms of my job, I'm older than some people twice my age. In terms of training, experience and vocation, I'm just the right age. Okay?

LIZ: *(to Peter)* Want some aloe vera for that burn?

ANAHERA: I'm sorry, I don't mean to be rude.

PETER: Don't be.

ANAHERA: People need to relate to me as my job, not my age.

LIZ: I'm just teasing him.

PETER: She loves it when I'm the least intelligent person in the room. I'm only here to make her look good.

LIZ: And you weren't rude. In fact, I think you have a great future ahead of you.

ANAHERA: Thanks, but we should talk about -

LIZ: Tell us something about yourself, take our minds off...

ANAHERA: We should talk about you two, and Harry and Imogen, not me.

PETER: It's good being distracted, to be honest.

LIZ: Is your family religious?

ANAHERA: It's not something –

LIZ: I know, but it's something to talk about, right?

ANAHERA: It's inappropriate for me to –

LIZ: Please. Just for a bit.

ANAHERA wavers, then decides she wants to help more than be appropriate.

ANAHERA: I was raised in the Ratana Church.

PETER: Okay.

LIZ: Wow.

PETER: I've heard of them, but I've got no idea what they believe.

ANAHERA: One of the things they don't believe in is spirits going along to doctor's appointments.

PETER: Want me to pass you the aloe vera?

LIZ: They don't believe in spirits?

ANAHERA: Or doctors much. They practise faith healing.

LIZ: You keep saying "they" like you're not part of them.

ANAHERA: It's tricky. I've been away for years. I go to the Temple when I'm back home, but...

PETER: Catholics call it "lapsed". Maybe you're a lapsed Ratana?

ANAHERA: Is that even possible?

LIZ: There's always a choice.

ANAHERA: If you've been soaked in a belief system all your life, you've absorbed it, it's a part of you, part of how you relate to the world, even if you don't realise it. You carry it around, like a stowaway.

LIZ: An unwanted pregnancy.

ANAHERA is surprised. It's not what she meant.

ANAHERA: I suppose.

11

PETER tries to make light of it.

PETER: Bit of a jump, Liz.

LIZ: Not really.

ANAHERA: Was one of yours unexpected? Harry? Or
  Imogen?

  A beat.

LIZ: Why did you do that?

ANAHERA: What?

LIZ: I didn't say "unexpected".

ANAHERA: I heard it.

LIZ: You changed it.

ANAHERA: But I heard it.

  *LIZ looks hard at ANAHERA but ANAHERA remains professional,
  open and strong.*

  The house phone rings. LIZ and PETER look at each other.

  PETER moves to answer the phone.

SCENE FUTURE NINE: IMOGEN THANKS ANAHERA

5pm, May, 10 years ahead

*IMOGEN strides into ANAHERA's office. ANAHERA (now 43) reaches
out her hand.*

ANAHERA: Hello.

  They shake hands.

IMOGEN: I'm Imogen. Thanks for seeing me. I know you're
  busy.

ANAHERA: No problem. How can I help?

IMOGEN: It's nothing really, I just wanted to – I'm amazed I was able to just walk in!

ANAHERA: We're here to help – it says so on the door.

IMOGEN smiles, gets the joke in the way it was intended. ANAHERA is good at putting people at their ease.

ANAHERA: Are you a client of ours?

IMOGEN: No. Well, we were, I suppose. Look, you probably don't remember me – I don't think we met – I was just a kid – but I've got a message from my mum. She wanted to thank you.

ANAHERA: That's nice of her. Thank you.

IMOGEN: You helped her, helped us, a long time ago. And she wanted to say thanks.

ANAHERA: You're very welcome.

IMOGEN: Because she didn't at the time.

ANAHERA: We see people in crisis. It's okay, really. And I really appreciate you passing on her thanks. How are you? Now, I mean?

IMOGEN: Great thanks. Just had a baby. A little girl.

ANAHERA: That's lovely. How old?

IMOGEN: 6 months.

ANAHERA: Where is she?

IMOGEN: Dunno. Playing in traffic, I guess.

ANAHERA doesn't over-react. She knows it's a joke. But IMOGEN, suddenly remembering where she is, immediately retracts.

IMOGEN: She's with her dad. In the car.

ANAHERA: *(smiling)* Probably not the best place to make jokes like that. And your mum? How is she?

IMOGEN: Dead. Thanks.

ANAHERA: I'm sorry.

IMOGEN: Me too.

ANAHERA nods, with a counsellor-empathy smile.

IMOGEN: A few weeks ago. She had another stroke. Probably a blessing, from her point of view.

ANAHERA: I understand.

IMOGEN: But before that, she told me she wanted you to know that she changed. After Harry ran away, after you came to our house, she – *(changed.)*

ANAHERA: Harry?

IMOGEN: Yeah, Harry.

ANAHERA: And you're Imogen…?

It all comes flooding back to ANAHERA. It's not an entirely pleasant memory.

IMOGEN: You remember us now, huh?

ANAHERA: Liz and Peter. My first solo.

IMOGEN: Was it? No wonder.

ANAHERA: I'm sorry.

IMOGEN: Don't be. You saved me.

ANAHERA: That's kind, but…

ANAHERA doesn't know how to describe how much of a failure she felt she was. For a moment, they are both back in the memory, placing each other in that memory.

IMOGEN: You can't save everyone. But you saved me.

SCENE PAST TWO: THE FILE.

10.15am, April, 10 years ago

The phone is ringing. We are back in the past.

PETER answers the phone.

PETER: Hello?… Not a good time. I have to keep the line free. I'll call you back.

PETER hangs up the phone.

PETER: Work.

ANAHERA: Is everything okay?

PETER nods.

PETER: The place can't run without me. I own my own business.

ANAHERA: I know. Roofing supplies. I've read your file.

There is a moment of silence as everyone, including ANAHERA, realises what she just said.

LIZ: We have a file?

ANAHERA: That's just what we -

PETER: We only called the police a few hours ago.

ANAHERA: All our clients have files.

LIZ: We're not your clients.

ANAHERA: Everyone we try and help – we gather as much information as possible, so that we can help as much as possible.

LIZ: So in the time between us calling the police and you arriving here, you wasted precious time creating a paper trail and researching our jobs and… what? What else did you find out about us?

ANAHERA: No, we didn't waste any time, we came as soon as we could. I just read the file in the car.

LIZ: A file that already existed?

ANAHERA doesn't want to answer. She is acutely aware she has broken protocol.

LIZ: Which is it? Did you waste time or did the file already exist?

PETER: Leave it, Liz. Does it really matter?

LIZ: Yes.

PETER: Who cares how they do their paperwork? This is about Harry.

LIZ: Which is it?

ANAHERA decides.

ANAHERA: Someone made a Report of Concern about your family. Ages ago.

LIZ: A Report of Concern? What is that?

ANAHERA: It's what we call it when -

LIZ: Someone made a complaint about us? Our children?

ANAHERA: It's not a complaint, it's a Report of -

LIZ: Who was it?

ANAHERA: We're not allowed to -

LIZ: When?

ANAHERA: A few months ago. That's why there was a file.

LIZ: But no-one contacted us. Have they?

PETER: Not me.

LIZ: So someone has phoned you -

ANAHERA: I know you must be anxious, but -

LIZ: I'm not anxious, I haven't done anything wrong.
    Whoever has accused me of -

ANAHERA: No-one has accused you of anything specifically.
    When someone raises a concern, it doesn't mean - look,
    the way we approach these situations is to work with
    people to make sure that children are okay. It's not about
    pointing fingers, it's about upskilling everyone.

LIZ: I have a Master's degree. I don't think I need upskilling.

PETER: Nothing was done, it was a prank call or something,
    I don't care. My son is missing and I couldn't care less
    about some curtain-twitcher with too much time on her
    hands.

LIZ: You're right.

ANAHERA: You're right. Harry is what matters.

LIZ: People are morons.

A silence.

LIZ: Coffee. Cake. That's what we need.

LIZ almost runs from the room.

There is an awkward moment.

PETER is uncomfortable.

ANAHERA feels this and deliberately calms herself in a professional manner. She breathes and adjusts her body language so it is peaceful, relaxed and open.

PETER heads to the sound system and turns on some music.

PETER: Can't stand the quiet. Makes me feel like someone's... *(died.)*

ANAHERA: Good idea.

PETER: I don't think I've ever noticed how loud that clock ticks. It was bloody expensive, but what a god-awful noise. Been driving me mad the last 20 minutes. Can you hear it?

ANAHERA: No. Not now.

She smiles at him.

He smiles back a small smile and turns the music up. He dances a bit.

From the depths of her bag, ANAHERA's phone rings. They both jump. The ringtone is annoyingly chirpy.

ANAHERA: Sorry, I thought I'd turned it off.

She grabs the phone from her bag. PETER scrambles to turn the music off.

PETER: Is it... *(the police?)*

ANAHERA: No. They'll ring you first, not me. But I'd better take this, it's Janet.

PETER: The emergency. No problem.

PETER busies himself around the room to give her some privacy.

ANAHERA: *(into the phone)* Hi Janet - *(Janet asks how it's going. Anahera darts a look back at Peter.)* Fine. When are you – ?

… (Janet's not coming back. Anahera covers her anxiety.) Okay, no problem. What's happening? *(Janet fills her in on all the details she couldn't say earlier in front of the Hunters; that a client family Anahera has been working with have seriously hurt their child.)*

ANAHERA turns her body away from PETER, trying to hide her reaction from him.

ANAHERA: Can you call me if anything...? … Yeah, I will. Bye.

ANAHERA hangs up. She tries to shake it off, struggling for self-control.

PETER: Are you alright?

ANAHERA nods her head, but it's patently not true.

PETER: Can I get you a drink?

With some effort, she pulls herself together. It's hard, but she does it.

ANAHERA: It's okay, I'm fine. Tell me some more about Harry. What TV shows does he like?

PETER is still concerned for her, but follows her lead.

PETER: Okay. No. No TV.

ANAHERA can't help but glance in the direction of the huge TV screen.

PETER: Well, we have a TV, yes, but you know...

ANAHERA: You limit your children's TV time? Many parents do.

PETER: True.

ANAHERA: An hour a day?

PETER: No. You'd need to check all that with Liz. She's the -

ANAHERA: I understand. She's the main caregiver.

PETER: And it's her… thing.

ANAHERA: She's the rule-maker.

PETER: She's great. The kids are great. We get so many compliments about them.

ANAHERA: Good on you.

PETER: I don't know how she does it. Some people think she's a bit strict, but the kids know where they stand, you know?

ANAHERA: Sure.

PETER: They know their place in the scheme of things.

ANAHERA: Right.

PETER: We had a kid here once who wanted to turn the TV on. Harry and Imogen both jumped up and said "Not for children!" So cute. Imi was still in nappies. "Not for children!"

ANAHERA covers her growing unease with a smile and an open statement. Social work 101.

ANAHERA: Parenting is the hardest job.

PETER carries on proudly, unaware. His family is awesome.

PETER: I'm pretty lucky. Liz makes it look easy. I'd say your job is harder. Going into all those tough families who get drunk and beat each other up and let the kids run wild.

ANAHERA: It's not all like that. It's mostly seeing what we can do to help. Educating people. Caring.

PETER: Frustrating though, yeah?

ANAHERA: Sometimes.

PETER: The light bulb has to want to change.

ANAHERA: Something like that.

PETER: Or there's no hope.

ANAHERA: There's always hope, but...

PETER: But?

ANAHERA: Sometimes it feels like we get there too late.

PETER: How do you mean?

ANAHERA: Like it was too late years ago, generations ago.

ANAHERA is clearly talking about something specific. The phone call.

PETER: You sure you're alright?

The house phone rings. LIZ rushes back into the lounge. PETER answers the phone.

PETER: Hello... Yes? ... Oh, thank God. *(To Liz)* They've found him.

SCENE FUTURE EIGHT: MURDER?

2am, October, 10 years ahead

(In the transition, LIZ, now 57, moves slowly and her body shows the signs of a recent stroke.)

It is dark. LIZ is asleep in her bed, alone.

HARRY (31) enters. He wears a brightly coloured knitted scarf.

HARRY stands for a moment watching her. He takes his scarf off and twists the ends around each hand, turning it into a garotte. He stands over her, unsure.

She wakes.

LIZ: Harry.

LIZ and HARRY lock eyes.

HARRY drops the scarf and walks away. For good.

LIZ sits up. Watches him go.

LIZ: Harry! Come back! Please!

SCENE PAST THREE: HARRY IS FOUND, BUT THE REACTION IS WRONG.

10.20am, April, 10 years ago

PETER is still on the phone, relaying the news to LIZ and ANAHERA.

PETER: *(into the phone)* Is he alright? … *(to the others)* He's fine.

ANAHERA: Thank goodness.

LIZ: He's okay?

PETER: He's fine, love.

LIZ moves away from the others, recovering her composure.

PETER: *(into the phone)* Can we - ?

PETER listens. ANAHERA watches and then moves to be near LIZ. She isn't quite able to touch her, though. She's not sure if LIZ would like it or not.

PETER: *(into the phone)* Thank you so much. See you soon.

PETER hangs up the phone.

PETER: They're bringing him here. Once the doc looks him over.

ANAHERA: Do you want me to drive you to him?

PETER: They said to wait here. By the time we got there, they'd be half way here. He's in Masterton!

LIZ: How the hell did he get to Masterton?

ANAHERA: All that matters is he's fine and he's coming home. It's over.

LIZ grabs her phone and checks her emails, glad that life can go back to normal.

PETER: It's over. Thank God. I should ring people. Excuse me.

PETER takes the house phone and leaves the room, already dialling.

ANAHERA watches him go. She turns back to LIZ, but she is engrossed in her emails.

ANAHERA watches LIZ for a moment, trying to think of the right thing to say.

ANAHERA: Shall we have some coffee while we wait?

LIZ doesn't answer. She's focusing on her emails.

ANAHERA: I can pour the coffees if you like?

LIZ looks up, like she'd almost forgotten ANAHERA was there. The trauma of the day has disappeared from LIZ's demeanour and we see the LIZ that her co-workers see. Cheerful, intelligent and hardworking.

LIZ: I have to get back to work.

ANAHERA: Now?

LIZ: My inbox is insane.

ANAHERA: Liz, no employer in the world would mind you taking the rest of the day off.

LIZ: I would, though.

ANAHERA: Seriously, Liz, you're exhausted. Wait until Harry gets home, spend some time with him, you need to -

LIZ: I'll deal with him later. The anticipation will make it all the better.

ANAHERA: It's a bit soon to be talking punishment, isn't it?

LIZ: Time for him to think about all the trouble he's caused.

ANAHERA: There might be a really good reason why he ran away.

LIZ: And for me to catch up on all this.

ANAHERA: He might be being bullied or something.

LIZ: 135 emails behind just because he's throwing a tanty.

ANAHERA: I don't think he's -

LIZ: It will take me days to get back on schedule.

ANAHERA: This is more important than -

LIZ: I need to not be here when he gets home because I might just kill him.

The words hang in the air, unable to be retrieved.

SCENE FUTURE SEVEN: SHE CHANGED.

11am, September, 10 years ahead

IMOGEN (mid-pregnancy) tucks a blanket around LIZ's legs.

LIZ: You will be fine, Imi. Everyone has a meltdown just before. It's normal.

IMOGEN: It's the hormones.

LIZ: Now you're minimising.

IMOGEN: You've had too much counselling, mum.

LIZ: Just because the feeling is "caused" by hormones, doesn't make it less real or less valid.

24

IMOGEN smiles.

LIZ: You'll be a wonderful mother.

IMOGEN: How does anyone know that?

LIZ: I've seen you with dogs. Your children will run you ragged and take shameless advantage of your good nature, but they will be the happiest kids on the block.

IMOGEN is pleased and comforted. She bustles around, taking nurse-like care of her mother, wiping her face, adjusting her clothes.

IMOGEN: Thanks.

LIZ: It's been a rough few months.

IMOGEN: I'm sorry I even started it.

LIZ: You didn't say much.

IMOGEN: It's worse now than it was before. Harry's worse than before.

LIZ: Maybe it has to be worse before it gets better.

IMOGEN: It was a stupid idea. DIY family therapy? What could possibly go wrong.

LIZ: Honey, you set up this whole family meeting thing, and you didn't say –

IMOGEN: It was meant to be a healing confrontation.

LIZ: Maybe you shouldn't have called it Armageddon, then.

A beat.

LIZ: You didn't say anything. Do you want to? We still can.

IMOGEN: It was a mistake.

LIZ: But you didn't say anything.

IMOGEN puts moisturiser on her hands and massages LIZ's stroke-affected hand as she speaks.

IMOGEN: Remember "Pilgrim's Progress"? How they carried their burdens on their backs? I think we unpacked all our burdens, flung them around the lounge at each other and now we're left standing in the mess. Like after a holiday, they won't fit back into the pack. And I wonder if we should have just dumped them, not even tried to unpack them, just dumped them and walked away.

LIZ thinks for a moment.

LIZ: He wasn't ready for that. I don't think he would have done it if you'd asked.

IMOGEN: I was talking about me.

A silence.

LIZ: I'm sorry.

IMOGEN: You said sorry for every single thing on Harry's list.

LIZ: I am sorry.

IMOGEN: But how can you be? You don't even remember some of them.

LIZ: He did though.

IMOGEN nods.

IMOGEN: How did it go last weekend?

LIZ: He just sat there watching sport. I tried to get him to talk but... Let me get us some lunch.

LIZ begins to get up from the chair.

IMOGEN: I'll do it, mum.

LIZ: I can do it, if you can stand waiting.

IMOGEN looks at LIZ, considering.

LIZ: Get some rest while you can.

IMOGEN: Take your time.

LIZ finally manages it, she stands.

IMOGEN: I don't have to leave, you know.

LIZ hobbles carefully towards the kitchen.

LIZ: You've taken enough time out of your life. You and Paul
need to start nesting.

IMOGEN: Okay.

LIZ: And I will keep on asking you if you want to say
anything. I'm not giving up on either of you.

LIZ turns back.

LIZ: I got her phone number. Anahera.

IMOGEN: Whoa. Did she remember you?

LIZ: I hung up before she answered.

IMOGEN: Wuss.

LIZ: I'll do it. I just wasn't ready.

IMOGEN: I'm joking. You don't have to ring her.

LIZ: I need to thank her. Should have done it years ago.

IMOGEN: She might not want to talk to you. You probably
ruined her career.

LIZ: She's a Lead Advisor at the Ministry.

IMOGEN: After what she did?

LIZ: I never told anyone what she did. I guess she didn't
either.

27

SCENE PAST FOUR: ANAHERA LISTENS TO HER GUT.

10.20 am, April, 10 years ago

ANAHERA takes out her notebook.

ANAHERA: Can I ask you a few questions? The more we know about how your family works, the better we can support you through the next few days.

LIZ: You've been wonderful, and I'm very grateful, but it's over now, and we'll be fine.

ANAHERA: How would you describe your parenting style?

LIZ: We can handle it from here.

ANAHERA: We're involved now. Let me help you. This will only take a few minutes.

LIZ decides it will be quicker to get it over with. She nods.

ANAHERA: How would you describe your parenting style?

LIZ: I don't know... Tactical warfare.

ANAHERA: Sorry?

LIZ: That was a joke.

ANAHERA: Oh. That's probably not the best idea.

LIZ: We work hard and we're okay financially, so the kids have everything they need. Is that what you mean?

ANAHERA: Would you say you're a strict parent or a liberal one? Do you have boundaries in place?

LIZ: Of course. My children are always being told how polite they are.

ANAHERA: That must be nice.

LIZ: It is.

ANAHERA: What about consequences? If they are naughty, what do you do in your family?

LIZ: The same as most people. Time out, extra jobs around the house, that sort of thing.

ANAHERA: Do you smack your children?

LIZ: Ah, the dreaded question.

ANAHERA: It's not illegal, depending on how it's applied.

LIZ: I know. I checked. And before you write anything down, I didn't say *I* dreaded the question. We actually don't smack much. We don't need to. They're mostly very well behaved. They do as they're told.

ANAHERA is about to ask another question, but LIZ interrupts.

LIZ: If it's not illegal, why do you ask that? Why's it even on your list?

ANAHERA: Part of my job is making sure people know that using "force for the purpose of correction" is unnecessary, and we ask a lot of questions so we can understand the family dynamic.

LIZ: They do as they're told. That's our family dynamic.

PETER comes back into the room.

PETER: I'm almost proud of him. Pretty amazing to have got that far by himself.

ANAHERA: True. It shows some enterprise.

PETER: Must take after his mother.

ANAHERA: Can we chat?

PETER: What about?

ANAHERA: What are your plans for when he gets back?

PETER looks to LIZ, who shrugs.

LIZ: She needs to complete her paperwork. *(to Anahera)* Which reminds me, first I'd like to clear up the little matter of that complaint. I want our "file" deleted, thanks.

PETER: Yeah, what was that all about?

ANAHERA: We can deal with that another time, once Harry is sorted.

LIZ: Someone has said something about me and I haven't had the chance to refute it.

PETER: It can't be much -

LIZ: We don't know that.

PETER: - or they'd have followed it up. We're saints compared to the ferals she normally deals with.

LIZ: I don't need to be compared to a feral in order to feel good, thanks very much.

PETER: I'm just saying we must be way down on the scale of things.

ANAHERA: Reports get triaged into "must be seen in x number of days". 1, 7, 28, etc. Sometimes the less critical ones aren't followed up.

LIZ: Good. Weeds out the time-wasters.

ANAHERA: But that doesn't mean that we don't take every Report seriously. Every child matters.

LIZ: Just tell us what it was and then we can all move on.

ANAHERA takes a breath, unsure.

LIZ: Put it this way, telling us now will save you a lot of time later.

It's a threat, albeit lightly said, but ANAHERA ignores it. She's playing her own game.

ANAHERA: Someone reported seeing a child standing in your back garden for a long time.

LIZ: How could they see into our back garden? Our fence is six feet high.

ANAHERA: I only know what the CSR wrote down.

PETER: The what?

ANAHERA: The Customer Service Representative.

LIZ: So no-one with any qualifications has even spoken to the person who made the complaint?

ANAHERA: It's not a complaint, it's a Report of Concern.

LIZ: Doesn't make it feel any less like a complaint. I work in a government department; once you get put on some file, you never get off it.

ANAHERA: Is there a reason why a child would be standing in your back garden?

LIZ: What's wrong with standing in the garden? It's a beautiful garden. Look.

PETER: It's one of our family consequences.

ANAHERA: Can you explain it to me?

LIZ: It's not complicated. It's like time out, except we don't let them have time out in their room.

ANAHERA: You don't want them to associate punishment with their rooms?

LIZ: The opposite. Their rooms are nice, comfortable. What kind of punishment is that? So they stand outside. Gives them a nice sense of scale too.

31

ANAHERA: Scale?

LIZ: Kids think they're the centre of the universe. Standing out in the middle of the garden helps them see how unimportant they are.

LIZ says this with a smile of collusion. She expects ANAHERA to understand and agree.

LIZ: That's why we get so many compliments about our kids. They're not as selfish as other children these days. They've been shown the bigger picture. You can have well-behaved kids without beating them to death.

Maia. ANAHERA catches her breath as a horrible image comes into her head. LIZ and PETER notice.

PETER: Both our families were pretty heavy-handed.

LIZ: *(a warning)* Peter.

PETER: I think it'll help her understand. *(to Anahera)* We made a conscious decision to parent in a different way than we were raised.

He is proud of himself and Liz. Meanwhile, Anahera has recovered.

ANAHERA: How long do they stand outside?

LIZ: Depends.

ANAHERA: But do you have a specific time attached to the consequence? You know, like a three year old might get three minutes.

LIZ: We don't have times. It depends what we're up to.

ANAHERA: What's the longest?

LIZ: It's always Harry. He's been harder to break than Imogen. I don't know if it's because he's a boy, or because

32

his character is worse, but in a way he's been a blessing because Imogen watches him and learns from his struggle.

The house phone rings.

PETER: Do you mind? It'll be work.

ANAHERA: No. Of course.

PETER takes the phone into the next room.

PETER: *(into the phone as he leaves)* Hello, this is Peter.

LIZ has quite enjoyed sharing her successful parenting strategies with ANAHERA, and is now charming and light-hearted.

LIZ: Are we done? I need to get ready for work now.

ANAHERA: But who will be here when Harry gets back?

LIZ: The police can drop him at school.

ANAHERA: They won't do that.

LIZ: The less fuss we make of him, the better, don't you think?

ANAHERA: They have to complete a proper handover.

LIZ: Then I'll pick him up from the police station and drop him at school. Happy now?

ANAHERA: Liz, I really feel this isn't the right way.

LIZ: I know what he needs and I will handle it.

Smiling at ANAHERA, LIZ heads out the door.

LIZ: *(calling as she exits)* Hey hon, are you coming in with me or shall we take two cars?

ANAHERA is alone – and lost. She gets her phone out.

SCENE FUTURE SIX: THE FALLOUT. ARMAGEDDON DIDN'T WORK.

2pm, August, 10 years ahead

HARRY and LIZ sit in armchairs in the lounge, watching telly. HARRY nurses a beer.

LIZ: Maybe we should have consulted a professional.

HARRY doesn't answer.

LIZ: They could have set it up like a proper family therapy session. Been our referee. Handed out the red cards.

HARRY doesn't laugh.

LIZ: They might have known how to get us from there to... somewhere better.

HARRY changes the channel a few times.

LIZ: Imogen should have -

HARRY looks sharply at LIZ.

LIZ: I'm not blaming her, it's just... It didn't work, did it?

HARRY doesn't answer.

LIZ: Armageddon didn't work.

HARRY: Nope.

LIZ: Is there any point me saying sorry again?

HARRY doesn't answer.

LIZ: I don't blame you.

HARRY: Can we just get through the weekend?

A silence.

LIZ: Thanks for coming. Imi hasn't been the same since...

HARRY: I wasn't doing anything. She needed a break from you.

LIZ: I'm worried about her. She doesn't look at me.

HARRY: She's been pretending everything's fine for 20 years. So, it wasn't a total failure. Now we can all stop pretending.

A beat.

HARRY: Did she say anything? After...

LIZ: Armageddon?

HARRY: Don't call it that.

LIZ: You two named it, not me.

HARRY: Makes it sound... sanctified.

LIZ: "Family meeting", then. Does it matter what we call it?

HARRY: Did she say anything?

LIZ shakes her head. A beat.

LIZ: She asked me to give you this. To say thanks for her weekend off looking after me.

She holds out a brightly coloured knitted scarf.

LIZ: She's been knitting for the baby.

HARRY gets up and takes it from her, puts it on.

He sits down and watches the television again, absent-mindedly playing with the scarf.

A silence.

LIZ: Do you remember that woman who came to our house?

HARRY: What woman?

LIZ: She was sent round when you ran away. She stood right there.

HARRY: I wasn't allowed in the lounge.

LIZ: I don't remember that.

HARRY: "Not for children." Remember?

LIZ nods.

HARRY: The dog was allowed in.

HARRY laughs.

HARRY: Imogen was right, I should have made a list. Here you go, mum, I forgot to mention this one: our family hierarchy. Dogs before sprogs.

LIZ waits for HARRY to look at her.

LIZ: I'm sorry.

HARRY: Yeah.

A silence.

LIZ: Do you really not remember her?

HARRY: Who cares?

LIZ: But she changed your life.

HARRY: She changed your life.

LIZ: And Imogen's.

HARRY: Yep.

LIZ: But not yours.

HARRY: Nope.

LIZ: Why? Was it because you were older than Imi was when we realised what we'd done?

HARRY: Or she's just nicer than me.

LIZ watches HARRY. HARRY watches television.

HARRY: She stank of piss. Anahera. Piss and self-righteousness.

He looks at LIZ.

HARRY: She had you on the ropes.

LIZ: You can say anything you want to me. Even now.

HARRY: It didn't help then, why would it now?

LIZ: Maybe Armageddon – *(Liz remembers he doesn't want her to use that word.)* that day - was just the start and we need to keep going, keep talking until –

HARRY: It's worse now than it was before.

LIZ: I'm sorry.

HARRY: It doesn't help.

LIZ: I'm sorry.

HARRY: Mum -

LIZ: I'm sorry.

HARRY stands up.

HARRY: Mum!

He goes to LIZ and leans right into her face. He almost whispers in her ear.

HARRY: I. Believe. You.

A silence.

HARRY: You've wet yourself.

LIZ: Yes.

HARRY: I'll get the stuff.

LIZ: I can wait. I don't mind.

HARRY: I feel nothing.

LIZ: I don't believe you. You're still angry.

HARRY: I don't care enough to be angry.

LIZ loses it.

LIZ: Aren't you tired of this?

HARRY: Yes.

LIZ: You need to forgive me! It's the only way you will feel better.

HARRY: It's the only way you'll feel better.

LIZ: No.

HARRY: You want me to pretend it never happened. Forgive and forget.

LIZ: No. Forgive and remember. As long as you forgive, you can heal. And then maybe Gina would take you back?

HARRY: Maybe I don't want her back.

LIZ: But -

HARRY: This isn't about me, it's about you. I want you to live a long life. Unforgiven.

LIZ: Will you forgive me when I'm dead?

HARRY: I don't know. We'll have to wait and see.

LIZ: I've changed. You know I have.

HARRY: So Imogen keeps saying.

LIZ: So why can't you... *(change?)*

HARRY: Your face is the same. I look at your face and I am
10 years old.

SCENE PAST FIVE: TAKING A STAND

10.25am, April, 10 years ago

ANAHERA dials Janet's number, trying to control her rising panic.

ANAHERA: *(into the phone)* Janet, when are you – *(The
answerphone kicks in. She waits for the message to play, then -)*
Janet, I'm with the Hunters and I ... There's something... I
think I need to do something, but... Please call me back.

*She hangs up. She stands in the middle of the lounge and tries to
calm herself. She shakes her hands out a bit. She closes her eyes. She
lifts her arms away from her sides and breathes deeply, in and out.*

PETER comes back in and notices what she's doing.

PETER: Is that the way Ratana pray?

He copies her posture.

ANAHERA: No.

They both stand normally again. It's a bit awkward.

PETER: Sorry, that was work.

ANAHERA: Peter, I need to talk about -

PETER: I've got to go in right away, I'm afraid.

He turns back towards the door, expecting her to follow. She doesn't.

PETER: Don't mean to hurry you, but... Are you waiting for something?

ANAHERA almost laughs, like he's solved it for her.

ANAHERA: Yes. That's it. Exactly.

PETER: *(with a smile)* You might have nothing else to do but chat, but I've got a busy day ahead.

ANAHERA: Can I just talk to you for a - ?

PETER: Not today. Make another appointment if you have to, with Liz, but right now -

ANAHERA: This is important.

PETER: Well, it'll have to wait for another time. Thanks for your help, though.

ANAHERA: I'm sorry, but we need to -

PETER: You've been great, but it's been an incredibly stressful day. Can we just go, please?

She doesn't.

ANAHERA: I don't think I can.

PETER: Am I missing something here?

ANAHERA: We haven't got to the bottom of it yet.

PETER: Of what?

ANAHERA: The issue.

PETER: What issue?

ANAHERA: The real issue. Underneath.

PETER: Harry? Don't worry about it. Everything's okay now. He's on his way home.

ANAHERA: I don't think he's okay.

PETER: Of course he is. They phoned. He's fine.

PETER really isn't listening, he grabs the door and flings it open.

ANAHERA: Not just Harry. Imogen too.

PETER: We're all fine, okay? And I really need to go. Now.

And finally she decides.

ANAHERA: No. I'm sorry. I'm not leaving. I can't.

PETER: You can't leave?

ANAHERA shakes her head.

PETER: Why not?

ANAHERA: I'm sorry. I have to do this.

PETER: Do what?

ANAHERA: Wait.

PETER: What the hell for?

ANAHERA: I'm not sure. Change. Insight... Change.

A silence.

PETER: What's your boss's phone number?

ANAHERA: It's on the card I gave you. Or you could ring her on my phone if you want?

ANAHERA holds out her phone. PETER looks at her like it's a bomb.

PETER: Is this some sort of test? Or trick?

ANAHERA: It's not a trick.

PETER grabs her phone, but doesn't know how to use it. ANAHERA offers her hand to help, but he moves away from her like she's

41

contagious. He goes to the sideboard and grabs Janet's screwed-up business card. He puts ANAHERA's phone down on the shelf, picks up the house phone, unfolds the card and dials the number on it.

PETER: Hello, this is –

He stops, annoyed. The answerphone. He hates being interrupted.

ANAHERA: I couldn't get through either.

PETER holds up his hand to stop her speaking while he waits for the message to finish.

PETER: This is Peter Hunter, I've got your office junior in my lounge and she seems to have forgotten where the front door is. I don't care what your "emergency" is, if you don't get her and her training wheels out of here pronto I'll be making an official complaint. Goodbye.

He hangs up, triumphant. PETER and ANAHERA look at each other. They both start to speak.

[ANAHERA: There is something -]

[PETER: You're insane if -]

They both stop.

ANAHERA: No, you go.

PETER: No, you first. I'm all ears.

ANAHERA: There is -

PETER: I can't wait to hear what you have to say to me. There's obviously something on your mind. So, why don't you just say it and then we can all get on with our lives while you take your judgemental superiority complex somewhere else. Somewhere that might believe that a baby social worker with a lot of book learning but no life experience could possibly have something useful to say.

42

ANAHERA: Is that how you parent?

PETER: What?

ANAHERA: If you don't get what you want, do you get sarcastic and then belittle your children?

PETER: You need to leave now.

PETER is physically intimidating. ANAHERA holds her ground.

ANAHERA: Do you bully them too?

LIZ enters wearing work clothes. She stops when she sees what PETER is doing.

LIZ: What's going on?

PETER doesn't move away from ANAHERA.

PETER: She won't leave.

LIZ: What?

PETER: She actually said she won't leave until we do something. Like she's trying to -

LIZ: Anahera, are you alright?

ANAHERA: Yes.

LIZ: Then what do you want?

ANAHERA: Something has to change.

LIZ: What?

ANAHERA: There's something wrong here and I don't know how else to help you see it.

LIZ: It doesn't sound like you're alright. Would you like me to phone your boss?

PETER: I've tried that. Listen, Liz, she's using us to make some sort of political point.

ANAHERA: Am I?

LIZ: Are you?

ANAHERA: I don't think so.

PETER: This is my house!

LIZ: Sit down, Peter.

PETER: What?

LIZ: Sit down.

> *They look at each other. They both know that LIZ will handle this better than PETER can. LIZ is giving PETER a way out and he takes it.*
>
> *PETER looks back at ANAHERA. He moves away, but doesn't sit down. His anger is still simmering.*
>
> *LIZ sets an alarm on her phone.*

LIZ: So, Anahera, what's up? I'll give you 20 minutes. We'll listen to you, and then you can leave. I think that's pretty generous of me, considering the situation. Alright?

ANAHERA: I don't know.

LIZ: You don't know much, do you? Have you even thought this through? Careful planning is vital for any successful venture. Just a quiet word in your ear, woman to woman.

ANAHERA: No, I mean, I don't know that I can agree to that. I don't have anything to say to you, because I don't think you'll listen. I don't need your 20 minutes.

LIZ: What do you want then?

ANAHERA: Insight. A sign of hope. Love. I don't know. I might not know until I see it.

LIZ: Look, I'm guessing this technique of yours isn't in the instruction manual. Once your boss realises you've gone rogue on her, here's how I think it'll go; she'll apologise, we'll get flowers and you'll get an official warning. Then you'll be put under supervision and given all the boring jobs until you get so disillusioned that you'll leave, which means they avoid any suggestion of unlawful dismissal. It's cruel, genius and common, believe me.

LIZ checks to see her message has got home.

LIZ: So, do you still think this is a good idea?

ANAHERA doesn't answer.

LIZ: Do you understand? You are wasting your time.

LIZ looks at PETER. Game, set, and match.

But ANAHERA isn't beaten. She looks at LIZ with a new thought.

ANAHERA: No. You're wasting time. This is a gift. I'm trying to give you something.

LIZ: No, you're like a telemarketer calling during dinner. Unwelcome, uninvited, unimportant.

LIZ goes to the door and opens it.

LIZ: So, now you understand, you can leave.

ANAHERA: I'm not leaving.

LIZ: You are, the only question is when. If you leave now -

PETER: Get out of my house.

LIZ: Peter. I've got this.

PETER: Some stupid girl who thinks she knows it all, coming into my house and looking at me like she's better than me. I just want to...

ANAHERA: Hit me?

PETER: I've already told you, we're not like that. Look around you for God's sake. Do we look like - ?

ANAHERA: Look at yourself. You're frightening. And I'm an adult. Imagine how scary you are to your children.

PETER: They know I won't hurt them.

ANAHERA: No, they hope you won't. The hit is still there, they can see it. You congratulate yourself for using words instead of your fist but your words have weight and your eyes are violent.

PETER: Oh, for - *(fuck's sake.)*

ANAHERA: You haven't hit me, but I'm still scared.

LIZ: Well, the sooner you leave, the sooner you won't be terrified.

ANAHERA: I'm doing this for you.

LIZ: You act like I'm some stupid abused wife who needs to be in a refuge somewhere.

ANAHERA: If you don't change, I think your children should be in a refuge somewhere.

LIZ: Is that a threat?

ANAHERA: I'm trying to - *(help you see.)*

LIZ: Because if it is, it's the most pathetic threat I've ever heard.

PETER: Our children are fine, they have a great life, they have all the right after school activities, they get good school reports, they'll go on to university and have great careers -

ANAHERA: But there is something underneath -

PETER: - so should I be apologising for giving them a great start in life and having high expectations of them?

ANAHERA: - underneath your expectations. A darkness.

LIZ: You're just embarrassing yourself.

ANAHERA: I don't know how to show you -

ANAHERA searches for the right analogy.

PETER: Because you're wrong.

She grasps the first one that comes.

ANAHERA: I was smacked as a child.

PETER: And now comes the sob story.

LIZ: I can't tell you how uninterested I am.

ANAHERA: My mum used to smack me around the legs with her hand. It hurt.

LIZ: So now you're getting revenge, are you?

ANAHERA: I used to say, "Never did me any harm".

LIZ: And now you've got a certificate in bleeding-heart, nanny-state nappy changing, you've changed your tune.

ANAHERA: No, it didn't do me any harm. But I've realised that's only because I know my mum loves me with a passion. And that's what I'm left with after the sting fades. The knowledge that I am loved, I am worthy of love.

LIZ: Does your boss know you approve of smacking?

ANAHERA: I didn't say I approve of it, I just think it's a more complicated issue than whether or not a parent smacks a child.

PETER: Hang on, so now you're saying it doesn't matter?

ANAHERA: I'm saying that the key thing is the love, not the smack, in terms of the outcome for the child.

PETER: So you don't care that we smack our children?

LIZ: Who cares what she thinks?

ANAHERA: *(to Peter)* <u>Do</u> you smack them?

PETER: I knew it. All a trick, eh? Soften them up, make them think you're on their side, then swoop in for the kill. Got a tape recorder hidden in your top?

ANAHERA: No. I just wonder why you'd lie about it, if you believe in it.

PETER: We haven't lied about it!

LIZ: You have no idea what it's like to be a parent.

ANAHERA: I never pretended I did.

LIZ: But you still think you can swan around offering impractical, untried advice like it's actually going to help.

ANAHERA: I don't think I've -

LIZ: Star charts and win-win situations. None of these things work in a real household. Where people are sleep-deprived and over-stretched and just hanging on, from one crisis to the next. There is no time to think, no time to negotiate, you go on instinct and you just keep one step ahead of them -

ANAHERA: Instinct? Or learned behaviour? Are you just doing what your parents did?

PETER: No! We told you that.

ANAHERA: You haven't changed anything fundamental. You're just doing the opposite of what your parents did. You're still stuck in their paradigm.

PETER: Paradigm. Jesus.

ANAHERA: You've changed the wallpaper, papered over the cracks.

PETER: No, I've had enough.

ANAHERA: Do you believe people are born bad?

LIZ: You need to leave.

ANAHERA: In your belief system -

PETER: Is she deaf?

ANAHERA: - does Harry need your help to grow into a good human being?

PETER: You need to stop talking now.

ANAHERA: Do you believe you have to beat the bad out of him?

PETER storms up to ANAHERA and shouts in her face.

PETER: GET OUT OF MY HOUSE!

ANAHERA is terrified, but holds her ground.

LIZ's phone alarm goes off. A beat.

LIZ calmly turns the alarm off.

LIZ: *(to Peter)* Imogen's got Girls' Brigade, so we'd better take both cars.

She touches him, kisses him, and moves away, gathering her things to leave. PETER, latching on to LIZ's calmness, regains his self-control.

PETER: Okay.

ANAHERA realises she's losing them. She scrambles for a new tack.

ANAHERA: 20 minutes? More like 5. Is that something you do a lot? Make an agreement then change the rules?

LIZ: Is this something you do a lot? Overstay your welcome?

ANAHERA: I've never done anything like this before. Doesn't that make it mean something more? It matters. Your children matter. More than my rudeness. It matters.

LIZ: I don't know what you think you're doing, but then I don't really care. You can let yourself out.

LIZ goes to the door, looks back at PETER, expecting him to be right behind her, but he's not. LIZ looks at ANAHERA.

LIZ: Enjoy your unemployment. Don't feel too bad about it. You just picked the wrong person. I always win.

LIZ exits.

PETER follows, but stands in the doorway for a moment, troubled. He shakes it off and exits, leaving the door open.

ANAHERA stands strong and silent, not sure what will happen next.

ANAHERA's phone rings. It's on the sideboard where PETER left it. Her impulse is to go to it, but she suddenly thinks it might be a trick to get her to move. She stays put. She looks around, wondering if the Hunters are watching her through the windows, testing her. The phone stops ringing.

She shifts her weight from one foot to the other and settles back to standing evenly on both.

The house phone rings. After four rings it switches to answerphone.

LIZ: *(voice message)* Hello, you've reached the Hunters. Please leave a message.

The phone beeps.

JANET: *(voice message)* Hello Liz and Peter, it's Janet from the support team. I've just got your message, Peter. Um, I'm so sorry, there's obviously been some misunderstanding between you... If Anahera is still with you can you please

pass on a message from me that we need her back here as
soon as possible.

ANAHERA is torn.

JANET: *(voice message)* If she's already left, then please accept
our apologies for the misunderstanding and let me assure
you of our continued support over the next few days. And
please don't forget to fill out the online feedback form
for our -

COLLEAGUE: *(in the background of the voice message)* Janet, the
hospital's on the phone. They're taking Maia into surgery
– *(right now.)*

*The sound is suddenly muffled and glitchy; Janet has quickly put her
hand over the receiver to protect client confidentiality.*

Janet removes her hand from the receiver, in a hurry to hang up.

JANET: *(into the phone)* I'll be in touch in a few days. Thanks.
Bye.

*The phone clicks and is silent. ANAHERA wants to grab her bag
and run, but she's is unsure what to do. She's made a stand now.*

*ANAHERA turns on her spot and takes in the whole room slowly.
Everything she sees confirms her decision. It matters.*

*As she stands facing outwards again, adult HARRY and IMOGEN
can almost be seen standing in the garden, waiting.*

*ANAHERA shakes her body out a bit, then stands in a relaxed,
strong pose. Eyes up, arms at her side. She takes a breath in, then
breathes out.*

She's staying.

END OF ACT ONE

Act Two

SCENE PAST SIX: WAITING.

11am, April, 10 years ago

ANAHERA stands in the same position.

ANAHERA's phone beeps. She shifts the weight between her feet, tempted.

A beat.

She hears a sound. Her first thought is that it came from the garden, but then she thinks it must be the Hunters returning.

ANAHERA: Hello?

> *She listens. Nothing.*
>
> *ANAHERA finds her equilibrium again and calmly stands waiting.*
>
> *(ANAHERA remains standing in her spot while the future scene develops around her.)*

SCENE FUTURE FIVE: LIZ AND IMOGEN ARE TOO CAREFUL WITH EACH OTHER: "SHE DOESN'T LOOK AT ME."

2am, Late July, 10 years ahead

LIZ lies asleep on her bed. IMOGEN enters quickly and quietly. She stops and stands (where HARRY stood holding the scarf.) watching her mother sleep.

LIZ suddenly notices IMOGEN and sits bolt upright in fright, which then freaks IMOGEN out. They both shriek.

When they calm down, it's awkward. IMOGEN doesn't look at LIZ.

LIZ: Are you alright?

IMOGEN: I'm fine.

LIZ: How long have you been standing there?

IMOGEN: I thought I heard something.

LIZ: What?

IMOGEN: Are you alright?

LIZ: I'm fine.

Neither of them can say what they're thinking. IMOGEN looks out into the garden.

IMOGEN: It must have been a cat.

LIZ: Probably.

IMOGEN: Or something.

LIZ: Yes.

A beat.

LIZ: Do you – *(want to talk?)*

IMOGEN: Ok then. Night.

IMOGEN leaves quickly. She doesn't want to talk. LIZ wraps the blanket tighter around herself. She won't get much sleep tonight.

SCENE PAST SEVEN: PETER LETS THE LIGHT IN.

Midday to Midnight, April, 10 years ago

ANAHERA waits alone.

PETER enters slowly and stands looking at ANAHERA.

PETER: You're still here, then.

ANAHERA: Yes.

PETER: What are you really doing?

ANAHERA: I'm making a stand.

PETER: But there's no-one here.

ANAHERA: I know. It's not going well, if I'm honest.

PETER: What do you want?

ANAHERA: I told you. Change.

PETER: Change.

ANAHERA: A change of perspective.

PETER: I don't understand how standing in our lounge will change anything.

ANAHERA: Nor do I.

PETER: Then why are you doing it?

ANAHERA shrugs. She's not sure she can make him understand.

PETER: I'm trying to help you here. I've walked off my anger, I've told work I won't be back for a bit. I want to help you. Liz will win, I can promise you that. And what about your job?

ANAHERA: I thought this was my job.

PETER: Maybe you're in the wrong game?

ANAHERA: Maybe. Why are you trying to help me?

PETER: Maybe we can help each other?

A silence.

PETER: Do you like your job?

ANAHERA: Yes.

PETER: But you don't trust it.

ANAHERA: What do you mean?

PETER: You're not following the rules. You're not doing it the way the others do it. Why?

ANAHERA: It's about you and your family, not me.

PETER: If that was true, you'd be following the guidelines, trusting the process. So something about your job, not my family, is why you're standing there.

ANAHERA considers this. He's got a point.

PETER: Is the job not what you expected?

ANAHERA: No.

PETER: How?

ANAHERA doesn't answer.

PETER: I want to help you. We can help each other. What have you got to lose?

ANAHERA: It's more than the job. It's the whole... I thought I would be more use. Some of them don't want to be helped, they want ... it's like they want things to change, but not themselves. They don't want to do anything differently, but they want things to be different. It's like I'm standing there with the answers written all over me, but they can't read them. They just look at me and go, what do you know, you've got a job, your parents have jobs, you don't know what it's like, you've got no kids, what the hell can you offer me? Book learning.

PETER is decent enough to look a little shamed. But ANAHERA isn't talking about him.

ANAHERA: But sometimes I look at a situation and I can see so clearly. But no matter what words I use, they can't see it. All they see is this golden land on the other side of some ghetto river. And they're so pissed off they don't live there, they can't see that I'm standing in front of them with a boat and a paddle saying, here you are, grab it with all your heart, paddle away, the golden land is just over there. But they look at me with resentment, they only want to go there if I paddle for them. And I would, if that would help, but it doesn't.

PETER: What happened?

ANAHERA: When?

PETER: You're not talking about us. It's someone else.

ANAHERA: No, I'm just -

PETER: That phone call earlier. Was it that?

ANAHERA looks at PETER for a moment.

PETER: What happened?

ANAHERA: We were too late. Generations too late.

PETER: For what?

ANAHERA: Maia. Three years old. Kicked so hard her liver split.

Another silence. ANAHERA is relieved to have told someone. PETER is genuinely appalled, but also confident he's now cracked ANAHERA and will be able to get her out before LIZ gets home.

PETER: That's horrible. No wonder you're upset.

ANAHERA: They're at the hospital now.

PETER: That poor kid... and I bet you want to be there too, right?

ANAHERA doesn't give anything away.

PETER: Look, I hope she'll be okay, of course… but surely this must make you realise how different we are?

ANAHERA: It makes it clearer.

PETER: You really think we have something, anything in common with someone who hurts their kid because the dole is a day late?

ANAHERA: Yes. That's why I'm standing here.

PETER: People like that, people who beat their kids, are low-lifes, with no education, druggies, deadbeats! Look around you! We're decent, hard-working -

ANAHERA: I'm standing here because you can't see it.

PETER fights back his annoyance, takes a breath.

PETER: What can you see?

ANAHERA: Hate.

PETER is shocked.

PETER: You think I hate my children?

ANAHERA: I don't know.

PETER: You're not making any sense.

ANAHERA: Your actions, Liz's actions, the way you talk about them. It's chilling. Like they're interfering in the smooth running of your lives, like they have no connection to you other than having to do stuff for them all the time. Like they're pets that you regret buying because you didn't realise what a pain it would be having to walk them every day.

PETER: I think you're just upset about that kid and you're taking it out on us.

ANAHERA: I'm not doing anything to you. That's the whole idea.

PETER: Doing nothing.

ANAHERA: And saying nothing – or trying to. Because it doesn't work.

PETER: Just because it didn't work for… what's her name?

ANAHERA: Maia.

PETER: Maia. You're taking one situation and applying it to every situation.

ANAHERA: You two are not going to get words. Especially not mine; that's obvious.

PETER: And you're offended.

ANAHERA: You would talk your way around any of my colleagues. No, what really matters is your children.

PETER: My well-fed, well-educated, warmly-clothed, non-injured kids that have a bedroom each and a family that – *(takes care of them.)*

ANAHERA: What family? Where are the aunties and uncles? The cousins? The grandparents? Who gets to see you all in private, when no-one's looking?

PETER: Just because you haven't met them, doesn't mean they're not there.

ANAHERA: But they weren't here. When Harry went missing. That's not – *(normal.)*

PETER: They didn't know – Liz didn't want to tell anyone until -

ANAHERA: Look at your photos. Just the four of you. All studio posed, no snapshots. Look at this house. Where's

58

the spare bedroom? Or a fold-down couch? Look at the
fridge. Where's the food?

PETER: You looked in the fridge?

ANAHERA: I wasn't snooping, I was making coffees. You're
alone. Your children are marinating in one flavour. And
it's bitter.

PETER: Hang on, aren't you judging us for being Pākehā?
Because we don't have cousins around all the time.

ANAHERA: I'm not saying you should.

PETER: Yeah you are, you're judging us against your set of
values and finding us lacking.

ANAHERA: I'm not standing here because you don't live with
your extended family. I'm standing here because my guts
told me something was wrong.

PETER: But are your guts telling you that we are raising our
kids in a way that doesn't feel right to you -

ANAHERA: Yes!

PETER: - because we have a different cultural outlook? A
different set of values.

ANAHERA: No. Of course not.

PETER: You can't judge another culture by your own
standards. It doesn't work that way.

ANAHERA: I'm not -

PETER: Like those women in North Africa lining up to have
their daughters' clitorises cut out and their vaginas sewn
up with a hickory twig.

ANAHERA: What?

PETER: I look at that from my cultural perspective and I think what kind of god-awful mother would do that to her child? But in their culture, they are helping their daughters succeed – to marry well – because no respectable man will marry a girl with normal genitals. In their culture, the good parents mutilate their daughters. And who am I to judge? See? Different cultures do things differently.

ANAHERA: Are you saying that all Pākehā leave their kids standing in the garden as punishment?

PETER: Perhaps different cultures value different things and their parenting reflects that. Perhaps Māori value connections, and perhaps we value self-reliance more.

ANAHERA: Perhaps. Is it about self-reliance though? Do you make them stand in the garden for their good or yours?

PETER: Both. Why is that a bad thing?

ANAHERA: Is it to foster self-reliance? Or is it to get compliments at church?

PETER: It's all of those things.

ANAHERA: If you were loving parents -

PETER: "If". Jesus -

ANAHERA: - who just had this one weird punishment, that might be fine, -

PETER: - you don't even think we're loving parents.

ANAHERA: - but this is about the sum of it all. Bruises fade, feelings tend to stay. It's the feelings under the way you parent.

PETER: I love my kids. How many times do I have to say it?

ANAHERA: Did you ever run away when you were a child?

PETER: Yes.

ANAHERA: How did your parents react?

PETER: I don't know. It wasn't a big deal. I told my mum I was running away and she packed me a lunch. I ran off down the road, no idea where I was going.

ANAHERA: What happened?

PETER: I went into my friend's back garden. I sat inside his playhouse and opened my lunchbox; honey sandwiches, squares of cheese and apple, and a bottle of juice. Best lunch ever. I felt free as a bird. When I finished I just got up and went home. Felt great.

ANAHERA: What did your mum do then?

PETER: Nothing.

He smiles, remembering.

PETER: She told me later she was hiding in the bushes, following me the whole time.

ANAHERA: Do you remember what you were angry about? Why you ran away?

PETER: No idea. I just remember the lunch!

ANAHERA: Did you ask her why she did that?

PETER: No. We didn't talk about – look, I just get on with things, you know? I don't go digging round looking for problems; if life is fine, then I let it be. Like my mum.

ANAHERA: She let it be, but she had your back.

PETER: 'Course she did! Doesn't mean -

ANAHERA: And underneath, you probably knew that. A deep sense of confidence that you mattered.

PETER: I've got my kids' backs! Anyone harms them, I'd kill the bastards!

ANAHERA: But what if it's you that's doing the harming? What if it's Liz?

PETER: You're seeing stuff that isn't there.

ANAHERA: No. You're not seeing. You're refusing to look under the surface, but the carpet is lumpy with all the stuff hidden under there.

PETER shakes his head.

ANAHERA: All I'm asking is that you lift up the corner and have a look.

PETER is unnerved by the challenge.

LIZ enters, sees ANAHERA and stops.

ANAHERA looks straight ahead.

LIZ: I've got to hand it to you. I'm actually a little impressed.

ANAHERA doesn't respond.

LIZ: There's a bit of backbone there, then.

There's no answer.

PETER: *(to Anahera)* I was really hoping we could sort this out between us.

ANAHERA: *(to Liz)* Where's Harry?

PETER glances out the window to the garden.

LIZ: *(to Peter)* I thought you had an issue with the Melbourne office?

PETER: I thought I'd try and fix this one first.

LIZ: Great. Now we've both altered our day for this.

PETER: Maybe that's a good thing.

ANAHERA: Where is Harry?

LIZ: You'll be thrilled to hear that the police agreed with you. They thought he should have a day off school, too. Do you people compare answers, or were you all taught from the same textbook?

ANAHERA: So he's here?

LIZ: I couldn't be bothered arguing.

ANAHERA: He's home?

ANAHERA looks to the door for HARRY to come in.

LIZ: Oh, he won't bother us in here. He's very independent. But he's safe, he's home, and now you can leave.

ANAHERA: I'm glad he's okay, but I'm not leaving.

LIZ: Really.

ANAHERA: Nothing has changed.

LIZ: In that case, we have three options: we ignore you until you give up; we call the police and get them to remove you; or we pick you up ourselves and throw you out with the other garbage.

PETER: I need some food.

PETER exits to the kitchen, leaving the door open. LIZ lifts her voice to talk to both PETER and ANAHERA.

LIZ: The third option is obviously my favourite, but it would only play into your hands. To make us the bad guys. But we're not going to fall for that.

PETER: *(off)* Let's just call the police, this is stupid.

LIZ: No.

PETER: *(off)* What?

LIZ: Ignore her.

PETER pokes his head around the door.

PETER: Liz.

LIZ: I thought I'd clean the kitchen cupboards, do you want to start doing the bathrooms?

PETER: We've already done that.

LIZ: The bathrooms?

PETER: Ignoring it. Hoping it will go away. It's still here.

LIZ: You prefer the police option? More bureaucracy, justifying our lives to people wearing cheap shoes?

PETER: I just want her gone.

LIZ: That's not really winning though, is it?

PETER: Jesus, Liz.

LIZ: Option 1 it is, then.

LIZ sits down and settles herself comfortably. She picks up a magazine and pretends to read it.

PETER: This isn't the same, love.

LIZ: Oh, I don't know.

PETER: Let's just call the police, pick up Imi and get takeaways.

LIZ: No. You go to work, then get Imi. I'll handle this. I'll text you when we're done here.

She's usually right, but he's not so sure this time.

PETER: Are you sure you want to do it this way?

LIZ: Her group is presenting tonight so you might want to run her through it a few times – and don't forget to take flowers for her to give to the leaders. Supermarket ones are fine. And then she's having a sleepover at Sophie's.

PETER gathers a few things from around the room - a coat, his keys, etc. He throws glances at LIZ to see if she's changed her mind. She doesn't look up from her magazine.

PETER leaves.

A silence. Broken only by the flick of magazine pages.

ANAHERA looks ahead. She sneaks a few eye-flicks, but LIZ doesn't react.

ANAHERA clears her throat. LIZ keeps turning the pages.

Time passes.

LIZ's phone beeps. She looks at it, smiles. (PETER has sent a quick "love you" while he's watching Imi's presentation.)

LIZ exits.

ANAHERA is alone. She rubs her legs and tries to shake them comfortable.

Time passes.

LIZ enters with air freshener, which she sprays pointedly around ANAHERA.

LIZ sits flicking through a different magazine.

Time passes.

Night is falling. LIZ turns lights on around the room, then exits.

Time passes.

LIZ enters with wipes. She spot-cleans a few areas. ANAHERA watches whenever LIZ turns her back.

ANAHERA's phone beeps. They both look at her phone on the sideboard. ANAHERA doesn't move. LIZ goes and gets it, brings it over and holds it up in front of ANAHERA's face.

ANAHERA struggles to control herself as she reads the text. It's from Janet. Maia is dead.

LIZ puts the phone back and exits, taking the wipes with her.

ANAHERA is alone with her grief.

Time passes.

LIZ's phone beeps. She enters and looks at it. (PETER wants to know what's taking so long – does she need his help?.)

Annoyed, she sends back a quick text. (No.)

LIZ exits.

Time passes.

ANAHERA is alone. Her legs are hurting.

LIZ enters, sits and watches ANAHERA, waiting for the break.

A muscle in ANAHERA's leg gives way and she stumbles. She can't stop a yelp of pain and shock escaping.

As soon as she hears it, LIZ begins speaking.

LIZ: Not long now then.

ANAHERA: I'm fine.

ANAHERA desperately rubs the cramping muscle in her leg.

LIZ: You're at the pain stage, your head is begging you to give in. This stage just depends on which is stronger in you; your head or your body.

ANAHERA: I'm fine.

LIZ: You forget I've done this before. Do you want to know which of my children has the stronger body or the stronger mind? Can you guess? You might be surprised.

This galvanises ANAHERA. She stands up straight.

ANAHERA: Thank you.

LIZ is annoyed at her tactical error.

LIZ: Take your time. I can wait.

ANAHERA: What are you waiting for?

LIZ: "I might not know until I see it."

Time passes.

LIZ is back in her chair. She watches ANAHERA struggle.

ANAHERA is finding it hard to stay upright.

PETER arrives.

LIZ: Didn't you get my text?

PETER ignores LIZ, goes straight towards ANAHERA.

PETER: This ends now!

But something stops him.

PETER and LIZ stare at ANAHERA as her bladder empties.

PETER is horrified.

ANAHERA collapses on the ground.

LIZ: Had enough?

PETER goes to help.

ANAHERA: Don't. Please.

PETER stops.

ANAHERA: I can finish this.

LIZ: I'll get you a towel.

ANAHERA: Thank you. That would be kind.

LIZ: No. This floor is bespoke. It cost a lot of money. That's not going to look great on your expenses sheet.

ANAHERA: I'm getting through to you, then.

LIZ: What?

ANAHERA: A while ago you would have offered me the insult before the towel.

LIZ looks hard at her and then leaves.

A beat.

PETER: Do you want a cushion?

ANAHERA: Have you ever offered a cushion to your kids? When they've been standing outside for hours?

PETER looks uncomfortable.

PETER: They love us.

ANAHERA: Ever seen a beaten dog snuggle up to its abusive owner?

PETER: Standing outside is not cruelty.

He doesn't sound as sure as he used to.

PETER: It's the same as time out.

LIZ arrives with towels, hearing some of PETER's words.

LIZ: Don't apologise for us.

LIZ tosses ANAHERA the towels, from a distance.

PETER: It's your thing, not mine.

LIZ: What is?

PETER: The thing I *wasn't* apologising for.

ANAHERA, with a towel around her waist, struggles to her feet again. She stands on another of the towels. LIZ and PETER notice but don't notice.

LIZ is focused on PETER – he won't look her in the eye.

LIZ: If you've got something to say, go ahead and say it.

PETER thinks for a moment, then finally looks at her.

PETER: I've been sitting in the car for hours. Thinking. And I keep coming back to it. Have I ever asked you for anything?

LIZ, cautious, doesn't answer.

PETER: To do something my way, to make me happy. I have never done it. Why?

LIZ: Because I have made your life so comfortable, you've never needed anything. It's always there before you need it.

PETER: It's because I don't know what I'd do if you said no.

LIZ looks at him and then looks at ANAHERA.

LIZ: She's got to you, hasn't she?

PETER: I love you. You're the most amazing woman, fearless, but -

LIZ: You think she's got a point.

PETER: You see? Fearless! LIZ: She's got to you.

PETER: Even if she's fired, we're screwed because there will an investigation and people always find stuff even if it's not there. The stupid standing outside thing will just be the start.

LIZ: I don't care what other people think.

PETER flicks a look at ANAHERA, which LIZ sees.

LIZ: I will get us through this.

PETER shakes his head.

LIZ: I will, you know I can do it.

PETER: I know, but I'm not sure that's - *(what I want.)*

LIZ: I love you.

PETER: I know.

LIZ: Then...?

PETER: Everything looks different.

LIZ: All of this is because of her? Standing in our lounge?

PETER: It's not about her. It's when I look back at... Do you... ?

PETER stops. He flicks another look at ANAHERA.

LIZ: She doesn't matter. Say it.

PETER: Do you like them?

LIZ: Them?

PETER: Our children.

LIZ doesn't answer.

PETER: Do you like them?

LIZ: I thought we were talking about – *(us?)*

PETER: They're part of it. Aren't they?

LIZ: You obviously think so.

PETER: I don't think you even... *(like them.)*

LIZ: Go on, just say what you have to say.

PETER: That's it. I've been thinking back over the years and...
It's as though you don't like them.

LIZ: Alright.

PETER: You don't like our children.

LIZ doesn't look away. PETER hadn't been sure until now.

PETER: You don't like our children?

LIZ doesn't look away.

PETER: You don't like our children.

LIZ: Not just ours. All of them.

PETER: Jesus.

They both look at ANAHERA. She keeps still.

LIZ: What matters is whether we're together on this. Are we?

PETER: I thought it was about bringing up children we could
be proud of, that it would be worth the not-so-good stuff in
the end.

LIZ: There's no point going any further if we're not together
on this.

PETER: It's different if that's not why you did it.

LIZ: Children are selfish. They need to be put in their place.

PETER: You punished him because his friend called our house.

LIZ: Phones aren't for children. They're not toys.

PETER: He didn't use it. His friend called him.

LIZ: He should have told his friend not to. You agreed with me -

PETER: It made sense at the time. So did "One smack for the child who did it, two smacks for the one who tells". Who is that for?

LIZ: Our children aren't tattle-tales, are they?

PETER: No. And we always get to finish our G & Ts.

LIZ doesn't answer.

PETER doesn't know what else to say.

LIZ: This is nothing new, I haven't hidden anything.

PETER: I know.

LIZ: Nothing has changed.

They both look at ANAHERA. The elephant in the room.

LIZ: I've never lied about it.

PETER: You look different.

LIZ: You saw me this morning. I'm the same person.

PETER shakes his head.

PETER: I let you handle everything because you're better at everything than me.

LIZ: Don't start with the self-pity -

PETER: It's a compliment.

72

LIZ: It's a cop-out.

PETER: No, I'm just saying I lost touch with what you were doing. It's my fault too!

LIZ: There is no fault!

PETER: I wanted well-behaved children too, but... it's not about that for you. It's about keeping them separate. Different rules for them, because they're not like us. They're barely human.

LIZ: Our children are an example to -

PETER: Our children are miserable!

LIZ scoffs.

LIZ: Oh, come on!

PETER: They're not well-behaved, they're bloody miserable!

PETER paces around the lounge.

LIZ: You're blowing this out of proportion.

PETER: I don't want this. I don't know what to do with it. *(to Anahera)* You started this. What can we do?

ANAHERA doesn't have a chance to answer.

LIZ: There's nothing wrong with us.

PETER: You don't like your children.

LIZ: Oh, they're mine now, are they?

PETER: Help me understand this!

LIZ: You'll feel better after you've had some sleep. This is all a delayed reaction to Harry running off.

PETER: But they're nice. Our children are nice. I don't understand.

LIZ: Nor do I.

PETER: How can you not like them?

LIZ: Oh for God's sake! It doesn't matter. I do the job, don't I?

PETER: The job?

PETER looks at LIZ.

PETER keeps looking.

LIZ reluctantly gives an inch.

LIZ: I can't help it.

PETER wants more.

LIZ: My mother shouldn't have had children and neither should I. But I did, and I've wanted to hand them back ever since. Apparently, you can't. Best to just get on with it.

(ANAHERA remains standing in her spot while the future scene develops around her.)

SCENE FUTURE FOUR: MID-ARMAGEDDON, GETTING SOME AIR

6pm, July, 10 years ahead

IMOGEN enters the garden in a rush, needing air and space.

She slowly breathes herself calmer.

She hears a noise inside and moves away from the door, wiping her face clean of the tears and snot. She stands looking out across the garden.

HARRY comes out with a beer. He's drunk, but not stumbling. He holds out his beer towards IMOGEN as a toast, but she doesn't turn round.

He walks away from the door in a different direction to IMOGEN.

Both would like to speak to each other about it, but it's impossible.

They stand looking out, at a distance from each other, trying to process it all.

HARRY: You realise I was just joking when I said we should call today Armageddon?

A beat.

HARRY: You got any other great ideas for family get-togethers? How about a nice visit to Auschwitz?

IMOGEN doesn't answer. HARRY looks around the garden.

HARRY: Where did you used to stand? Here? Here?

She doesn't answer, but she can't help looking at the spot. HARRY takes a swig.

HARRY: I used to mix it up a little. See if Mum noticed.

He laughs a bit. Maybe tries a few different spots to stand. Then he finds his spot, <u>the</u> spot. He stands still for a moment, remembering how he felt as a child.

HARRY: Gina tried to start a garden at our place. I mowed it flat.

He swigs the last of the beer.

HARRY: We should go back in. She might think we've run away, and call the police.

IMOGEN doesn't respond, but it's clear she's not keen. She breathes deeply, like she can't get enough oxygen.

Finally, she turns and looks at HARRY. They can't quite meet eyes.

75

IMOGEN: This is awful.

HARRY agrees. IMOGEN turns and goes inside.

HARRY: Ding ding ding... round 2.

HARRY follows her in.

SCENE PAST EIGHT: PETER BACKS AWAY.

12.30am, April, 10 years ago

ANAHERA, LIZ and PETER are in the same position as before.

PETER: I need time.

LIZ: We can work this out.

PETER: No. I don't mean you-and-me us, I mean all of us.

LIZ: If we can sort us out, the rest will follow. We just need to support each -

PETER: We need to do what's best for them.

LIZ: Children are resilient, they'll cope as long as we lead the way.

PETER: I think we should do what's best for them, not us.

LIZ: Why? What makes them more important than us?

PETER: More important?

LIZ: They have to fit in with us, not the other way round.

PETER: But we have a choice, they don't. If I walk out of here right now, no-one is going to bring me back against my will.

LIZ: Who'd want to leave here? You and I would have killed for a home like this when we were kids.

PETER: But I can if I want. I can earn a living, do what I want, and not have to ask anyone's permission.

LIZ: Because you're an adult. You've earned it.

PETER: Our children have no choice. They have to live here. They *have* to snuggle up...

He realises he's using the words ANAHERA used.

PETER: They have to snuggle up like a beaten dog snuggles up to the owner who just kicked it, in order to survive. They put up with it because what other choice do they have? Oh my God.

PETER goes to leave.

LIZ: Where are you going? You were there every step of the way, you were right beside me.

PETER: Yep. Enjoying my easy life. I need time to think.

He goes to leave again.

LIZ: This is stupid, just because I'm not the mother of the year. It doesn't matter. They don't matter. They take and take, and expect everything to revolve around them, and they won't even be here in a few years, they'll leave home as soon as they can and they'll never call. They don't matter. I matter! You have to stay and work this out with me.

LIZ goes to PETER, touching him, trying to appeal to him.

LIZ: We're a team, we're invincible, we're bulletproof.

PETER holds her at arm length.

PETER: Don't.

LIZ ignores him. She is all over him, touching and kissing him.

77

LIZ: Peter, I can change, whatever you want, just don't go.
I can do it, you know I can.

PETER holds himself stiff and unresponsive – the physical silent treatment.

They are frozen for a moment in a one-sided embrace.

PETER removes her hands from his body.

PETER: I can't...

PETER leaves.

LIZ tries to hold it together, but she crumples in on herself, until she is on the ground. She can't breathe.

ANAHERA is horrified. This is not what she intended.

ANAHERA reaches towards LIZ, to comfort her. Without looking up, LIZ stops her.

LIZ: Don't.

ANAHERA waits, unsure what to do. LIZ curls into a foetal ball.

(ANAHERA remains standing in her spot while the next scene develops around her.)

SCENE FUTURE THREE: ARMAGEDDON.

2pm, July, 10 years ahead

In the same configuration as the three people at the start of the play, IMOGEN sits on the couch where ANAHERA sat, HARRY paces up and down near the window, and LIZ sits in her chair. The coffee table is covered with empty beer cans and a few wine bottles. They've been here for a while.

No-one speaks for a bit. No-one can quite look at each other. Finally, LIZ, the bravest, speaks.

LIZ: What else?

No-one answers.

LIZ reaches awkwardly for her glass. It's empty. HARRY notices and automatically moves to fill it up for her, but stops himself, cross with himself.

IMOGEN empties the bottle dregs into LIZ's glass.

A beat.

LIZ: Is there any more?

HARRY: *(deliberately misunderstanding)* Wine?

LIZ: On your list.

HARRY: I had no idea you could drink so much. I'm almost proud.

LIZ: It's a gift.

She raises her glass in a toast to her ancestors' mighty livers and takes a swig.

LIZ: Keep going.

HARRY: Shouldn't I be feeling better by now?

He laughs and drinks more. So does LIZ.

LIZ: I know there's more. I can take it.

HARRY: Bully for you. I need a break. Does this thing still work?

HARRY picks up a remote and turns on some music. He stands at the window and looks across the garden to where he would have stood as a child.

LIZ: We should keep going. Get it all out.

LIZ darts a look at Imi. Imi keeps her head down.

LIZ: Let's recap. I hit you. Hard and often. I'm sorry.

HARRY turns the music up a bit. LIZ continues. As usual she is the bravest in the room.

LIZ: Around the body. The face. And I wore big rings that hurt you when I backhanded you. I'm sorry. I didn't allow you to have friends over to our house. I'm sorry.

HARRY turns the music up louder. IMOGEN, upset, moves away.

LIZ: I broke your toys or threw them out as punishment for breaking things or being messy. I'm sorry. One time I beat you with wooden hangers for damaging some dried flowers. I'm sorry. I held you up to ridiculous standards. I'm sorry. I embarrassed you by belittling you in front of other people. I'm sorry.

HARRY keeps turning the music up and LIZ has to get louder to be heard over it. IMOGEN covers her ears.

LIZ refuses to give in to tears – she doesn't want them to think they should feel sorry for her – and carries on.

LIZ: I made you stand in the garden for hours. I'm sorry. I locked you out of the house all day in the school holidays. I went on overseas holidays without you, I did dreadful things and stupid things and insane things and I am so, so sorry.

LIZ is shouting "SORRY" when HARRY suddenly turns the music off.

A silence. IMOGEN is a ball of pain at the edge of the room.

HARRY: None of that matters.

LIZ: It matters and I am sorry.

HARRY: Those were just things that happened. I'm not standing here because of the shitty things you did. It was the undercurrent. Living in that permanent fog of dislike.

Knowing you are unwelcome. Knowing at bone level
that you don't matter, you have no rights and no worth.
It changes who you are. Who you become. Who you have
to become to survive. You chipped away at me until all
I had was anger. And now I don't exist except when I'm
angry. I can't hold my children because the softness I feel
terrifies me. My throat is raw from holding back what
I feel for them and I push them off my lap rather than
feel that sadness.

LIZ: I know. That's how I felt about you.

HARRY looks at LIZ, then at IMOGEN, who started this whole mess.

HARRY: How is this supposed to make me feel better?

No-one has an answer.

SCENE PAST NINE: THE MIDDLE POINT (THE LOWEST POINT.)

2am, April, 10 years ago

Time has passed, but no-one has moved. LIZ is still crumpled on the ground. ANAHERA is still unsure how to handle this.

ANAHERA decides. She takes a step.

LIZ: Uh-uh.

ANAHERA stops.

LIZ: Where are you going?

ANAHERA: You need help.

LIZ: No.

ANAHERA: Please. Let me get – *(someone.)*

LIZ: Stay.

ANAHERA: I'm not a therapist.

LIZ: You started this, and you need to -

ANAHERA: I don't have the training.

LIZ: You think?

ANAHERA tries a different approach.

ANAHERA: What about God?

LIZ: What about Him?

ANAHERA: You haven't mentioned God lately. It might help.

LIZ: I haven't mentioned breathing either, but somehow it's
    still happening.

ANAHERA: Maybe this is the time to lean on your faith.

LIZ: Praise the Lord and pass the ammunition.

ANAHERA: What?

LIZ: That's my faith.

ANAHERA: I don't understand.

LIZ: Family saying. It means...

She trails off, exhausted and frustrated.

ANAHERA: Are you alright?

ANAHERA goes to move again.

LIZ: I said stay.

ANAHERA: Okay.

LIZ: No. Not okay. My life was perfect.

ANAHERA can't reply – their ideas of perfect are so far apart.

LIZ: My life was perfect.

LIZ gets up off the floor.

ANAHERA: It can't have been.

LIZ: And you broke it.

ANAHERA: Not if your children were miserable.

LIZ: You have shattered my life into a thousand pieces. In one day.

LIZ stalks towards ANAHERA.

ANAHERA: He's angry, I know, but there's still – *(hope.)*

LIZ: Stomped all over it with your big clumsy feet.

ANAHERA: Liz, I didn't mean –

LIZ explodes in ANAHERA's face.

LIZ: So you don't just get to just walk away like you had nothing to do with it. Do you understand?

A beat.

ANAHERA: I don't know what you want.

LIZ: If you didn't know what you were doing, you shouldn't have interfered.

ANAHERA: I didn't know this would happen.

LIZ: Thrashing about blindly with your theories and your gut-feelings.

ANAHERA: I'm trying to help your children.

LIZ: Children are parasites, they do what they need to do to survive. Babies smile at 6 weeks so we don't kill them.

ANAHERA: Is that what you did? As a child?

LIZ: Nice try.

A silence. ANAHERA desperately searches for a way to reach LIZ.

ANAHERA: I wanted to help. That's all. I still do. And I don't understand why it's so hard for you to let me help you.

LIZ doesn't respond.

ANAHERA: I still can. I'm good at it. I taught Maia to use words. I only spent two afternoons with her but I taught her to say "yes" and "no". And I think I can -

A dreadful thought hits ANAHERA. It resounds around her head a few times before she says it out loud.

ANAHERA: I taught her to say "no".

This gets LIZ's attention.

A silence, while the full realisation hits ANAHERA; what might have caused Maia's father to kick her to death.

LIZ watches ANAHERA's pain, unmoved.

LIZ: So, we're not the only family you've helped today then?

ANAHERA is speechless.

LIZ: Your mother must be so proud.

ANAHERA: *(more to Maia than Liz)* I'm sorry.

LIZ rounds on her.

LIZ: No. You wanted to be the one to save us all.

ANAHERA: I'm sorry.

LIZ: You thought you could ride in on your white charger and save us from ourselves. You haven't saved anyone.

ANAHERA: I'm sorry.

84

LIZ: It doesn't help. Nothing you do will help. Harry will grow up and destroy his children, just like me, and Imogen's breastmilk will be bitter and her children will be starved and needy, just like mine.

Silence.

LIZ: Stay. Go. I don't care.

ANAHERA is lost. LIZ withdraws.

LIZ: I'm tired.

(LIZ and ANAHERA remain while the next scene develops around them.)

SCENE FUTURE TWO: HOPE ON THE ROAD TO ARMAGEDDON.

10am, July, 10 years ahead

IMOGEN and HARRY are taking a break on the journey to LIZ's house.

IMOGEN: You ready? Shall we go?

HARRY: Not yet, eh?

IMOGEN: She'll be watching the road for us.

HARRY: Just give me 5.

IMOGEN: You alright?

HARRY: Yeah. I could throw up though.

IMOGEN: Yeah, I couldn't eat breakfast.

A beat. HARRY deliberately changes tack.

HARRY: I've made a will.

IMOGEN: Right.

They both gladly slip back into their jokey demeanour – their usual way of relating to each other.

HARRY: I've told my boss he can have my knives and my recipe file. I've cleared out the chocolate wrappers and the sex toys from my bedside table.

IMOGEN: Me too.

HARRY: It's only fair to those we leave behind.

IMOGEN: I've cancelled my gym membership.

HARRY: I've had KFC and jelly beans for my last meal.

IMOGEN: Too far.

HARRY: Fair enough.

IMOGEN: I've put shitloads of alcohol in mum's fridge.

HARRY: In vino veritas?

IMOGEN: One way to get you both in the same room.

HARRY: Clever.

IMOGEN: And obviously I've put deadbolts on all the doors so you can't do a runner.

HARRY: You run away one time, and they never let you forget it.

IMOGEN: I'm glad you did.

HARRY: Actually, I didn't run away.

IMOGEN: What?

HARRY: True.

IMOGEN: So... the police just showed up for the hell of it?

HARRY: I mean I didn't plan it or anything. I just started walking. One moment I was standing in the doorway, the next I was walking. Out the gate, down the road. I just kept going.

IMOGEN: Nice.

HARRY: Yeah, it was. Free.

IMOGEN: Until they found you.

HARRY: Kinda.

IMOGEN: You never ran away again, though?

HARRY: Nope.

IMOGEN: Was that because it got better?

HARRY: It didn't get better.

IMOGEN: Of course it did.

HARRY: It got different.

IMOGEN: She changed.

HARRY: Yes, she changed. Give her a freakin medal.

IMOGEN: And you never ran away again.

HARRY: I wasn't "found". I chose to come home. I practically ran into the police station.

IMOGEN: Why?

HARRY: Because I was stupid, because I was a kid, because it wasn't fun sleeping rough? Take your pick.

IMOGEN: You're too hard on yourself.

HARRY: No, I basically chose to live with that woman. It was shit, but it was easier than not. Middle-class white boy liking his comforts. You can imagine how good I feel about that.

IMOGEN: Is that why you never gave her a chance? Because you felt guilty or something about coming back?

HARRY: Jesus, Imi, I don't bloody know. I try not to think about it.

They think their own thoughts for a moment.

IMOGEN: I ran into Mrs Gilbert yesterday. She says hi.

HARRY: Did you tell her what we're doing?

IMOGEN: We were in the supermarket. It didn't seem right.

HARRY: "Morning Mrs Gilbert, we're off to see mum to discuss all the dreadful things she did to us when we were kids and you were just over the back fence congratulating yourself on what lovely neighbours you had."

IMOGEN: It wasn't just her. All the adults around us just let it happen. No-one challenged them.

HARRY: And you continue to be angry with the wrong people. Mrs Gilbert didn't do anything wrong except not notice.

IMOGEN: People should notice and do something.

HARRY: And you should be angry with the right people.

IMOGEN: I'm just willing to share the blame around. You like to keep it all for one person. You don't even blame dad.

HARRY: I do -

IMOGEN: He was there the whole time.

HARRY: - but there's no point being angry with a dead man.

IMOGEN: Do you still think she killed him?

They burst out laughing.

HARRY: I'd forgotten that.

IMOGEN: You had me worrying about that for years.
Whenever I had a fight with a boyfriend I'd check the
brakes on the car before I stormed off. Kinda ruined the
drama, but you have to run with what you know.

A silence.

IMOGEN: Do you know what you want to say?

HARRY: Kind of.

IMOGEN: I don't think this'll work if you don't get everything
out. The whole idea is that we get it all out so it stops
festering under the surface.

HARRY: What do you actually want to achieve?

IMOGEN: I want us to create new memories.

HARRY is about to mock the idea, so she talks before he can speak.

IMOGEN: Not making up new ones to paper over the old.
If we do this properly, get it all out, deal with it, then
the next step is we all spend time together doing normal
family stuff; outings, meals, changing the furniture round.
Lots of short visits where nothing remotely tense occurs.
Eventually we'll build up a store of new memories; the
old stuff won't be hanging in the air between us all the
time. There will be new old stuff. "Remember the time we
blah, blah" Fun times, disagreements, but no left-overs,
no echoes. That's what I want. Family. What are you
hoping for?

HARRY: I'm hoping to drink like a bastard. No kids this
weekend.

A beat. IMOGEN doesn't let him off the hook.

HARRY: Alright. I'm hoping it might lift this weight on my chest. Do you get that? Like someone sitting on you?

IMOGEN nods.

HARRY: What are you going to say?

IMOGEN: I've got plenty to say.

HARRY: Really?

IMOGEN: Screw you.

HARRY: What?

IMOGEN: I was there too. Just because I love the woman now doesn't mean I loved her then. She was just as much of a bitch to me as she was to you.

HARRY: This is what I don't get.

IMOGEN: What?

HARRY: So how can you even look at her?

The atmosphere has changed. They can't look at each other.

HARRY: Seems like a lie.

IMOGEN: You've never understood because you've never tried to understand. I've got plenty to say.

A beat.

HARRY: No, I'm trying, but that just doesn't make sense. If you've got issues with her, why do want her in your life? In your child's life?

IMOGEN: It's not that simple.

HARRY: I've never left mine alone with her.

IMOGEN: I know. You think she doesn't know? It kills her.

HARRY: And we're back to it being about her. Who cares what she thinks. This is the consequence, you know? She brought this on herself.

IMOGEN: But I didn't.

HARRY: What do you mean?

IMOGEN: You're like this black fog hanging in the air between us. When I come in the door, she looks past me. To see if you've come too. And when you look at me, you see her. Admit it. You both look straight through me. And you know what? I didn't do anything wrong. I didn't hurt you and I didn't hurt her. But you're both still so stuck in your battle, and because of that, I don't exist.

HARRY: You exist! You're the one playing happy families!

IMOGEN: So why is it still all about you two? I made peace but the war is still going on around me, so obviously my peace doesn't matter. I don't matter.

HARRY: You matter.

Silence.

HARRY: But you might be asking a bit much of one afternoon.

Silence.

IMOGEN: We should get going. She'll have the kettle on by now.

IMOGEN leaves. HARRY follows more slowly.

6am, April, 10 years ago

Dawn. The room slowly gets lighter as the sun rises. They are exhausted and have been silent for hours, neither sleeping. LIZ suddenly speaks, startling ANAHERA.

LIZ: Your mother smacked you.

ANAHERA: Yes.

LIZ: You still love her?

ANAHERA: Yes.

LIZ: Why?

ANAHERA: She loved me more than she smacked me.

A beat.

LIZ: They are all I have left.

ANAHERA: Sorry?

LIZ: If he doesn't come back, they are all I have.

ANAHERA finally loses her temper.

ANAHERA: They don't exist for your benefit! Damaged people like you shouldn't be allowed to have children.

LIZ: Finally!

ANAHERA: The damage just gets passed down through the generations, getting worse and worse until someone gets kicked in the liver and dies.

LIZ: Haere mai, the true Anahera.

ANAHERA: How will you feel when that happens? When Imi beats up her daughter because you didn't break the cycle, you just passed it on down the line.

LIZ: I already know how it feels.

ANAHERA: But you can change, you have time. She's only 7.

LIZ: I am beyond redemption.

ANAHERA: No one is.

In a heartbeat, ANAHERA knows that's true for herself as well.

ANAHERA: And I will stand here until you believe it.

LIZ: The Bible says if I've imagined something, then I've done it.

ANAHERA: I believe you can change.

LIZ: Go and ask Harry if I've kicked him in the liver this week, because I've sure as hell thought about it.

ANAHERA: I will stand here until you believe you can change.

LIZ: Your effort was wasted. No one was saved. You are not a saint and I am beyond redemption. You could have stood here for a year and you wouldn't have got what you wanted. What was it? Insight. Love. Change. Love.

A huge new thought. LIZ chokes on it.

LIZ: Oh my God.

ANAHERA: Are you okay?

LIZ: Oh my God.

ANAHERA: What is it?

LIZ: Change. I remember. It was different. I felt different.

ANAHERA: It's okay, Liz.

LIZ: When he ran away.

LIZ calls out.

LIZ: Harry! Come in here.

ANAHERA: Don't wake him up.

LIZ: Do you see? I felt different.

ANAHERA: Liz, we can sort this, we don't need to wake him.

LIZ: He's not asleep.

ANAHERA: How do you - ?

LIZ: Harry! Come inside.

ANAHERA: Inside?

LIZ: Now!

ANAHERA: Oh my God.

ANAHERA runs out to find HARRY.

LIZ: Harry! Come here now!

LIZ can't keep still, she squirms around the room, waiting for HARRY and ANAHERA.

She remains in motion while the next scene develops around her, the past and the future existing in the same space and moment.

SCENE FUTURE ONE: PLEASE COME TO ARMAGEDDON.

6pm, June, 10 years ahead

HARRY arrives, closely followed by IMOGEN. Simultaneously, LIZ (in the past) restlessly waits for ANAHERA to return with HARRY.

IMOGEN: We're worried about you.

HARRY gives her a withering look.

IMOGEN: I'm worried about you.

HARRY: And you think sitting in a circle and rehashing the past until we can all have a group hug is going to fix it?

IMOGEN: Can't make it worse, right?

HARRY: Hippie.

IMOGEN: I want this baby to grow up in an awesome family.

HARRY: You're three minutes pregnant. It's not even a kidney bean yet.

IMOGEN: That gives us some time then.

HARRY: I'll be an awesome uncle! Just you wait.

IMOGEN: No, I mean a whole family. Christmas, Easter, birthdays. I want the whole deal.

HARRY: You've already got it.

IMOGEN: Not without you there too. Will you do it?

HARRY: Leave it alone, Imi. It's not brilliant, but we get by.

IMOGEN: No. Something's got to change. And she's willing.

HARRY: You've already spoken to her about it?

IMOGEN: She really wants to sort it out too. She's in boots and all.

As HARRY absorbs this information, the past scene continues simultaneously.

SCENE PAST TEN (CONTINUED.): THE ONLY WAY IS UP

6am, April, 10 years ago

and

SCENE FUTURE ONE (CONTINUED.): PLEASE COME TO ARMAGEDDON

6pm, June, 10 years ahead

ANAHERA enters from the kitchen. LIZ looks beyond her, but HARRY doesn't come in.

LIZ: Harry, come in here.

　A beat.

ANAHERA: He's getting a drink.

　　HARRY: She wants to do this?

LIZ: I need to talk to him.

　　IMOGEN: Yes.

ANAHERA: You left him standing out there all night?

LIZ: Yes.

ANAHERA: And before then?

LIZ: Yes.

　　　IMOGEN: Please? Just think about it. Now she's had
　　　the stroke you don't need to worry that she'll beat
　　　you up.

ANAHERA: When?

LIZ: Since he got home. He stood there nearly as long as you.
Harry, come here.

HARRY: I don't know.

ANAHERA: He's tired.

LIZ: I need to talk to him. It's different now.

IMOGEN: Wouldn't you like some peace?

LIZ: I need to tell him. Bring him in.

ANAHERA: I don't trust you.

LIZ: It was different. When he ran away. Like I'd banged something, but it hurt somewhere else. Change, but not; it was already different. You see? I must have always felt like that about him.

IMOGEN: So?

LIZ: And I need to tell him.

IMOGEN: Will you come?

ANAHERA: Let's both go. We can make him some food.

LIZ: He needs to come to me.

ANAHERA: Liz.

HARRY: She should really come to me, you know.

LIZ: He needs to come to me, not the other way round.

ANAHERA stares at LIZ for a moment, then walks out.

IMOGEN: Might as well go back to the scene of the crime. Poetic justice, or something. So…?

LIZ gets herself into a commanding position on stage.

LIZ: Harry, come here.

He doesn't arrive. LIZ fights down her anger – she wants to change, but it's not that simple. She veers wildly between imperious and vulnerable/true. Both feel wrong now.

LIZ: *(More gently.)* Harry?

> HARRY: Okay.

> IMOGEN: Really?

IMOGEN throws herself at HARRY and they hug each other.

> HARRY: It can't get any worse, right?

LIZ: Harry, I missed you. When you ran away, I missed you.

He doesn't arrive.

LIZ: Harry? Did you hear me?

HARRY leaves IMOGEN and walks across the stage.

LIZ: Harry!

> IMOGEN: You won't regret it!

HARRY waves, exits.

HARRY is gone.

LIZ: Harry! Come back. I love you.

He doesn't come back.

IMOGEN is happy, filled with hope for the future.

> IMOGEN: Yes!

THE END

Production notes

There are aspects of story and character that are left unexplained in the script of Anahera. However, for actors and directors working on the play, I've included some notes below to clarify my intentions.

Anahera is not a saint and Liz is not a monster. Peter is as guilty as Liz. All the characters lie. And Imogen's story is the centre of the play because she represents hope for the future.

Liz

Liz is a survivor; intelligent and resilient. She was raised by a cold, abusive mother, and she has worked hard to rise above her traumatic childhood. She has mostly succeeded. To her friends Liz is witty, charming and fun to be around, even though they probably feel slightly inadequate in comparison. Most people only get glimpses of the steel underneath. Liz isn't evil, she's damaged.

Peter

Peter's explosive, bullying father terrified him as a child, but his mother loved him dearly. Peter is less damaged by his childhood than Liz, but he has a sense of entitlement to a good life because his childhood was tough. Peter is an equal in his marriage and in the abuse of the children. He was happy to go along with Liz's parenting style it because it worked, and it was easy for him. He believes he is a loving parent, but in fact he is barely a parent. His children have little impact on his life; they have been trained to be low maintenance. He views himself as a good, hardworking, decent bloke (he is only some of those things), and when he realises what he's done, the shame overwhelms him. But, crucially, he runs rather than face the consequences.

Their relationship

Liz often tells Peter what to do and he often does what she says, but he is not dominated; he AGREES to it. They are equal partners, he hasn't given away his power, this is the way their great relationship works. Peter provides Liz with the unconditional love she never experienced as a child, and in return Liz does all the emotional labour at home, including decision-making. Liz's guiding principle has always been to keep Peter happy, to ensure he keeps loving her. He feels he deserves the awesomeness that is Liz.

Their parenting
They have no qualms about their parenting but equally they're not stupid, they know they're out of step with the world. They are not afraid of Anahera's judgement of them, their perfectly behaved children are proof that their methods are fine. So, at first, when Anahera refuses to leave, the problem from their perspective is purely Anahera-in-their-lounge, not what she's saying. It is only much later, alone in the car, that Peter allows himself to think about what she has said.

In performance
In the first scenes, the audience should believe they are watching a normal family coping with the disappearance of a child. Any odd statements or unusual reactions should appear as an understandable reaction to stress. Clues in the script need to be carefully played so the audience isn't aware too early that there is something wrong about this family. If there's a choice between playing a line ominously or lightly, choose lightly for as long as is possible. Anahera begins to sense the undercurrent, and so will some of the audience, but it needs to not be overt. These early scenes are also the only chance the audience has to see Peter and Liz as their friends might see them and it is important to ensure this happens. The longer the audience can believe that Liz and Peter are normal parents (just like us), the better. It will make the truth all the more devastating once it is revealed.

Anahera's stand
Once Anahera decides to make her stand, it is important that she does not move from that spot until the end of the play. She is a pou; rooted in the ground, supporting the framework, and holding the space in between for the family. (She doesn't necessarily know that's what she's doing.)

WWW.OBERONBOOKS.COM